The EU Budget

THE EU BUDGET

RESPONSIBILITY WITHOUT ACCOUNTABILITY?

GABRIELE CIPRIANI

CENTRE FOR EUROPEAN POLICY STUDIES
BRUSSELS

The Centre for European Policy Studies (CEPS) is an independent policy research institute based in Brussels. Its mission is to produce sound analytical research leading to constructive solutions to the challenges facing Europe today. CEPS Paperbacks present analysis and views by leading experts on important questions in the arena of European public policy. They are written in a style geared to an informed but generalist readership of policy-makers, government officials, academics, civil society and corporate executives.

The opinions expressed by the author in this publication in no way commit the European Court of Auditors to which he belongs. The author gratefully acknowledges insightful comments as well as helpful research and editorial assistance received, which have greatly contributed to this book.

JEL Classification: H2, H5, H6, H7

Keywords: European Union, Fiscal Policy, EU budget, Fiscal Federalism

ISBN 978-94-6138-053-1

Centre for European Policy Studies
Place du Congrès 1, B-1000 Brussels
Tel: 32 (0) 2 229.39.11 Fax: 32 (0) 2 219.41.51
e-mail: info@ceps.eu
internet: http://www.ceps.eu

To my parents

CONTENTS

List of Boxes

List of Figures

List of Tables

PREFACE

EU funds do not come for free. European citizens contribute to the EU budget through general taxation; thus, the EU and its member states compete for the same revenues. Since resources are limited and are needed for many essential purposes, there are opportunity costs. It is therefore necessary to make choices transparently, to prioritise action and to give account for the use of citizens' money.

An adequate accountability process for EU funds is not only instrumental to good management; it is also a critical condition of legitimacy for public authorities. In its conclusions on the budget guidelines for 2011, adopted on 16 March 2010, the Ecofin Council acknowledged that the EU budget is "one of the most significant tools to guarantee the accountability of the European Union towards its citizens (...); an accurate and accountable use of the EU resources is one of the essential means to reinforce the trust of the European citizens."

This study aims to shed light on the thorny question of holding to account for EU funds. Starting from the concept of accountability and the fundamentals of the EU framework, it examines the existing accountability arrangements (by whom and how, for what, to whom) within the role-sharing between the European Commission and the member states. It endeavours to explain the reasons for and the consequences of diffused responsibilities and of the resulting accountability gap. Finally, the study sketches a possible scenario for the future, with two main characteristics: an interpretation of the concept of European added-value based on limited and achievable objectives and one single accountability framework.

Gabriele Cipriani
November 2010

EXECUTIVE SUMMARY

How, for what and to whom are the European Commission and the member states of the European Union to hold accountable for the some €120 billion spent each year by the EU budget? What are the main factors that lie at the root of the accountability gap? What is a possible way out?

The EU budget accountability gap

This study asserts that there exists an accountability gap, which can be attributed to three main reasons. First, due to opaque revenue arrangements, citizens are not directly made aware of the more than €200 each of them pays on average each year into the EU budget. Therefore taxpayers are not induced to attempt to exert democratic control over the use of EU funds. Secondly, EU objectives are grand and numerous, with no clear or specific expected achievements. Vague expectations are easier to report but harder to be held accountable for. Finally, most of the management functions are carried out by national bodies that are not directly accountable at EU level and over which the Commission has no authority, although it is ultimately responsible for the budget's implementation. Responsibilities remain diffused and there is no single owner of the EU budget. *Ex-post* clearance has become for the Commission a shortcut for accountability, thus putting the focus on compliance of spending rather than on 'value for money' requirements.

The current accountability gap affects the significance of the discharge procedure before the European Parliament, through which citizens exercise their right of scrutiny.

A possible way out

The accountability gap is a symptom of the difficulties that have prompted the current EU budget review process. A new concept for the EU budget must go hand-in-hand with appropriate institutional reform, setting governance and administration of the budget by intentional action, i.e. according to well-defined EU objectives.

The EU budget is *one* of the 28 EU public budgets and *one* of the tools available to the EU. This means that, as for any EU action in accordance with the principle of subsidiarity, the EU budget's aim should be to do things that nobody else can (or will) do with better results. It is about achieving objectives of common European interest, which is more than simply transferring money across member states. This leads to the concept of EU added-value, with three main characteristics: *catalytic* (making something happen that would otherwise not happen or happen more slowly), *targeted* (concentrating on the best added-value and most effective results on the basis of evaluation and impact assessment) and *realistic* (drawing from J. Monnet's 'balance-sheet of needs and resources'). The underlying logic is: Why Europe?

A more selective definition of the EU added-value would imply less numerous objectives than at present and more precise (measurable) targets. In turn, this would make it possible to concentrate the resources on a limited number of spending programmes, thus ensuring a critical mass to produce visible results. The EU budget should provide the 'cake' rather than the 'icing'. EU funds should be linked to outputs, outcomes and impacts rather than to inputs of eligible spending. Performance should be rewarded and sunset clauses should provide for a discontinuation of spending programmes that fail to show meaningful results after a certain period of time. Also, a shift from inputs of eligible spending to results will make it possible to define control systems in a broader perspective, taking account of 'value-for-money' concerns and thus enhancing their added-value for the management.

The overall size of the EU budget ought naturally to be determined by the sum of the costs of the various objectives assigned. Whereas an overall ceiling on EU revenue could still be maintained, the introduction of a genuine EU tax should be considered. It would seem logical that the effort to make visible the achievements of the EU budget is accompanied by a corresponding visibility of the costs incurred.

Since it is about achieving EU objectives, implementation should follow a political mandate given to the European Commission. The budget implementation should take place under its full responsibility as the 'executive' of the Union. Like today, role-sharing between the EU and national levels seems necessary, but in a different framework. Management functions would be delegated to national bodies according to programmes' needs, on the basis of some form of 'contract' based upon pre-specified outputs and performance targets as well as budgetary allocations. This delegation should be made conditional on these bodies passing beforehand a 'stress test' aimed at establishing their capacity to manage public funds effectively. Partnership with national bodies should involve co-decision for management choices. This means putting an end to the dissociation of the decision-making aspect from the financial implementation. The Commission will therefore take up the role of the 'programme manager', having both the authority over trustful delegated bodies and the legitimacy to put in place the necessary measures to achieve the intended objectives.

The Commission would ultimately be accountable before the European Parliament not just for compliance but also for the extent to which the expected results were achieved, the contribution made by activities and outputs of the programmes to the outcomes, and the learning and change that have resulted. Thus the discharge procedure will be given full dignity, providing opportunities for redress and better management.

Overview	
Status quo	**Proposal**
Revenue provided by national contributions and consequent 'fair return' logic	An EU tax, made directly visible to citizens
An overall spending ceiling, to which a plurality of spending programmes should adjust, with a lack, for most of them, of the necessary critical mass to produce recognisable results (the 'icing' rather than the 'cake')	An overall spending ceiling as a result of a limited number of catalytic, targeted and realistic spending programmes, with sufficient funding to achieve visible results (the 'cake' rather than the 'icing')
Spending based on eligible items and absorption of funds as an implicit target	Spending made conditional upon pre-defined outputs, outcomes and impacts, with both performance and sunset clauses
National bodies designated by member states	'Stress tests' on designated national bodies to be accredited by the Commission
Separation of financial implementation (Commission) from management decision (member states)	One single management process under the Commission's authority as programme manager

1. RESPONSIBILITY & ACCOUNTABILITY

The buck stops here.

Attributed to former US President Harry S. Truman

There are many examples of early accounting systems and forms of accountability among individuals as well as between them and the state, particularly within the ancient cultures of Mesopotamia and Egypt. One can find for example in the Code of Hammurabi, thought to be the most complete record of ancient law, the formulation of the principle of accountability through the example of a builder. If a builder undertakes to build a house for some one and, even though it is not yet completed, the walls seem to be in danger of toppling down, the builder must make the walls solid from his own means.[1]

Evidence has been found in ancient civilisation of accounting methods comparing expected and actual performance, based on a number of detailed entries in the accounts showing a careful division of labour, allocation of predetermined work targets, regular reporting on actual achievements and the remainder of work to be completed (Carmona & Ezzamel, 2005:18).[2] There is also evidence of a reward structure taking account of the rank of every category of work, hierarchical position or responsibility.

A Biblical statement of accountability can be found in the detailed accounting statement of the funds collected for the erection of the Holy Sanctuary and of the various materials used for its furnishings and vessels.[3] Referring to the Christian tradition, St. Luke tells the story of a rich man who had a steward who was reported to him for squandering his property. He summoned him to prepare a full account of his stewardship. Notably, the rich man concluded: "No servant can serve two masters. He will either hate one and love the other, or be devoted to one and despise the other".[4]

Accountability: *'E pluribus unum'*

Accountability is a key component of good governance. As a basic principle of public life, no authority should be exempt from scrutiny or review by others and someone has to be held to account for the results. Indeed, "[s]ociety has the right to ask a public official for an accounting of his administration".[5] Despite differences in legal traditions, constitutional structures and governance systems, accountability has emerged over time in EU member states (and indeed in constitutional democracies) as one of the shared principles for public administration and its relations with citizens.[6]

Effective accountability arrangements generate a supervision process, aiming at improving quality in decision-making and providing the means for correction, prosecution and redress (Sigma, 1999:25). Bovens (2007:192,193) indicates four reasons for the need of public accountability: taxpayers' democratic control over public policies; integrity of public governance against corruption, nepotism and abuse of power; improved performance of public funds; and maintained or enhanced legitimacy of public governance.

Accountability is undoubtedly a kind of catch-all term with several faces: a good synonym would be "answerability" (Starling, 2008:169; Bovens, 2007:185) or responsiveness. van Gerven (2007:1,2) identifies different dimensions for accountability (legal, ethical, political and financial) and attributes to the concept a double meaning: "accountability for" (to be called to account, for example for incorrect behaviour) and "accountability to", that is being obliged to inform someone, for example Parliament. This difference could also be described as "giving an account" and "holding to account".

In public life, "giving an account" basically consists of disclosing information in public and providing adequate justifications, but not necessarily to face consequences. The matters to account for have chiefly to do with how well the principles embedded in administrative law are honoured by civil servants and public authorities on the one hand, and on the other, about how well the legal procedures for shaping public administration decisions are followed (Sigma, 1999:13,19).

"Holding to account" goes beyond the mere provision of information. The concept stems from the expression primarily used in a principal/agent context.[7] It implies that the policies, decisions or actions are explained, motivated and argued before Parliament.[8] The more so when decisions are taken on the basis of discretionary elements. "Holding to account" entails a relationship with another entity that has the authority to impose sanctions or give rewards. In this respect accountability could be defined as "a relationship between an actor and a forum, in which the actor has an obligation to explain and to justify his or her conduct, the forum can pose questions and pass judgment, and the actor may face consequences" (Bovens, 2006:9).[9]

The difference between "giving account" and "holding to account" sheds light on the difference between "responsibility" and "accountability", two words that are often used interchangeably due to some conceptual overlap.[10] In its essence, "responsibility" refers to holding a specific office or duty and it is about working within prescribed tasks, frameworks and standards. Accountability is about ensuring that responsibilities are actually carried out (one cannot expect rules and requirements to be self-enforcing!) and that action is taken where they are not. Therefore, accountability trumps responsibility.

A clear identification of responsibilities and a deep sense of it is a necessary, though not sufficient condition for accountability. More importantly, if "responsibility" can be (and often is) shared, "accountability" cannot without the risk of being voided of its inherent value, thus creating the conditions for a "no man's land". To capture the concept of several responsibilities resulting in one single accountability, one could refer to the motto "*E pluribus unum*", out of many, one.[11]

Finally, the accountability process is closely linked with the exercise of power and the legitimacy of policies - and those pursuing them (Bemelmans-Videc & Lonsdale, 2007:3). It is about taking decisions and as such it implies the authority to put in place the necessary measures towards the expected targets. Supervision and a sense of ownership represent a first condition to make sure that public bodies are performing their functions effectively and efficiently (Sigma, 1999:11, 13). Accountability implies awareness of what is done, how well it is done, how much it costs and who paid for it (Bird & Smart, 2001:16). The concept goes hand in hand with transparency (Dyrberg, 2002:83). Two other vital factors are rewards and sanctions.

Accountability and public funds

Public administration is increasingly expected to manage public funds in accordance with the principles of economy, efficiency and effectiveness.[12]

The accountability process is meant to pro-actively enforce these principles, by achieving intended results and preventing abuse of public powers and mismanagement of public resources (Sigma 1999:22). All naturally, audit institutions strive for full accountability. For example, the mission of the General Accountability Office (GAO) of the United States government is "to help improve the performance and ensure the accountability of the federal government for the benefit of the American people".[13] Concerning the EU budget, the European Court of Auditors promotes accountability and transparency and assists the European Parliament and Council in overseeing its implementation.[14]

The Auditor General of Canada has defined accountability as "a relationship based on obligations to demonstrate, review, and take responsibility for performance, both the results achieved in light of agreed expectations and the means used".[15]

The accountability process can be summarised by the activities diagrammed in the following figure.

Figure 1. The accountability process

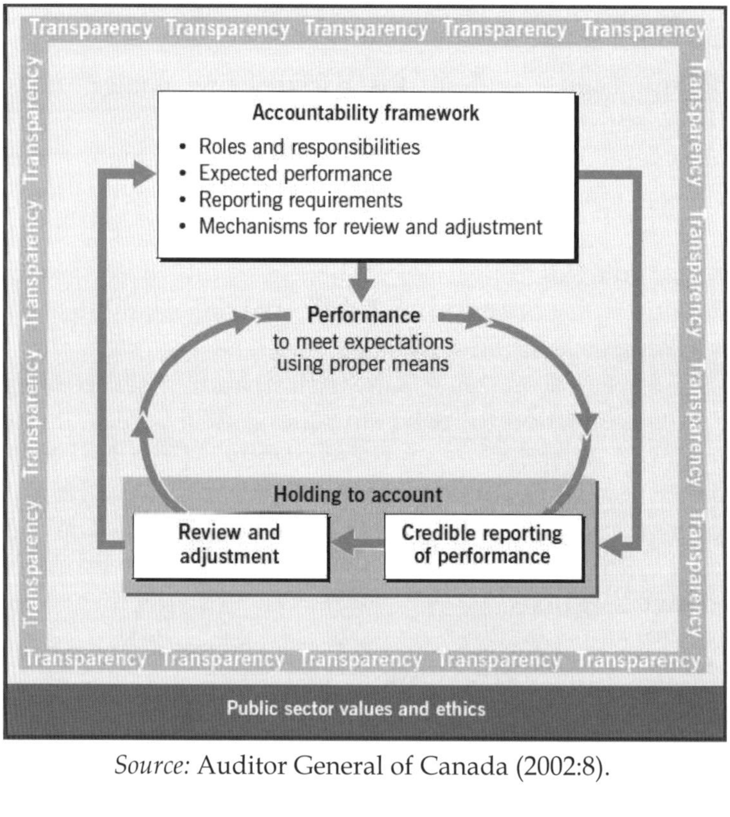

Source: Auditor General of Canada (2002:8).

The effectiveness of the whole accountability process depends on the set-up of this framework and on how those responsible are held to account. In particular, a proper accountability framework requires:

- a clear understanding of the roles and responsibilities of all parties concerned;
- expectations that are mutually understood and realistic;
- the identification of what information is to be reported by whom to whom and when; and,
- clarity on how and by whom performance will be reviewed and adjustments made.

This is of the outmost importance when, as a result of numerous partnerships involved, the accountability process becomes diffused and it is difficult for citizens to identify the ultimate responsibility.

Holding to account is based on credible reporting and (as a prerequisite for) review and adjustment. Conditions for a credible reporting requires being able to convincingly demonstrate, through external auditors' assessment of the fairness and reliability of reported information:

- the extent to which the expected results were achieved;
- the contribution made by activities and outputs of the programme to the outcomes;
- the learning and change that have resulted; and
- the soundness and propriety of the means used.

This means that credible reporting is not possible if expectations are unclear, in particular as to how the outputs produced are expected to lead to the desired outcomes. Vague expectations are easier to report against but harder to be held accountable for.

Review and adjustment close the accountability loop. They require that those responsible for reviewing performance should consider what results have been accomplished in the light of expectations and of circumstances, recognising both achievements and failures as well as putting in place the necessary corrections.

Finally, there are two key sustaining elements for the accountability process. First, openness and transparency. They imply that one can see clearly into the government's activities, particularly regarding performance. Second, the effectiveness of the accountability process depends very much on promotion and enforcement of public sector values and ethics, such as fairness, honesty, probity, integrity and fidelity to the public trust.

The EU 'fundamentals'

The European Union originates from member states' choice to pool aspects of their respective sovereignties, by conferring to the Union powers to act independently "to attain objectives they have in common" through the EU institutions.[16]

The Union's objectives are far-reaching. It is about promoting peace, its values and the well-being of its peoples; to offer EU citizens an area of freedom, security and justice without internal frontiers; to establish an internal market for the sustainable development of Europe; to promote scientific and technological advance; to combat social exclusion and discrimination, and to promote economic, social and territorial cohesion, and solidarity among member states; and to establish an economic and monetary union.

These objectives are pursued "by appropriate means commensurate with the competences",[17] according to a three-fold 'steering compass'. First, the principle of conferral sets the boundary on the Union's action "within the limits of the competences conferred upon it by the Member States in the Treaties to attain the objectives set out therein".[18]

Then, concerning the use of these competences, the principles of subsidiarity and proportionality come into play.[19] The subsidiarity principle, applicable in areas of shared competence with member states, requires one to demonstrate that member states cannot sufficiently achieve the objectives of the proposed EU action, which can rather, by reason of its scale or effects, be better achieved by the Union.[20] One of the characteristic of EU actions is therefore to be 'inevitable' in view of reaching a better result. Finally, "the content and form of Union action" should be limited to "what is necessary to achieve the objectives of the Treaties" (principle of proportionality).[21] See Box 1.

The underlying logic is that for every EU action one should be able to answer convincingly the question: Why Europe?

Box 1. The principles of subsidiarity and proportionality

The principle of subsidiarity requires one to establish that the objectives of the proposed action cannot be sufficiently achieved by member states' action in the framework of their national constitutional system. The reasons for concluding that an EU objective can be better achieved by the Union must be substantiated by qualitative or, wherever possible, quantitative indicators. Subsidiarity implies weighing up all kind of advantages and disadvantages, and finally the exercise of political discretion. It is a dynamic concept, which allows EU action to be expanded where circumstances so require, and conversely, to be restricted or discontinued where it is no longer justified.

The principle of proportionality is about the intensity or nature of the EU's action, which shall not go beyond that which is necessary to achieve the objectives of the Treaty. EU measures should leave as much scope for national decision as possible. Consideration should be given to setting minimum standards, with freedom for member states to set higher national standards. Any decision must favour the least demanding option. This means in particular that, in its right of initiative, the Commission must: consult widely before proposing legislation; justify that a legislative proposal complies with subsidiarity and proportionality; explain whenever applicable the reasons for the financing of an EU action in whole or in part from the EU budget; and, finally, minimise and make proportionate to the objective to be achieved any financial or administrative burden falling upon the Union, national governments, local authorities, economic operators and citizens.

The European Union is neither a classical international organisation nor a state: "[p]eople have frequently stressed the innovative nature and the special balance of the Community edifice, which organises not the separation but the sharing of powers".[22] Indeed, this edifice is founded on the principle of representation of interests, not on the principle of separation of powers 'à la Montesquieu' (Lenaerts, 1991:12-14).[23]

Functions that are exercised at the national level by the government are, at EU level, a matter for the EU legislative and the Commission, whereas the implementation of policies is largely delegated to national and regional administrations. The Union has no administration at individual country level and therefore relies on each member state to implement its decisions. The EU administration is in fact a chain of national administrations (Sigma, 1998:13).

The European Union does not fit within 'conventional' governing structures and cannot therefore be squeezed into a narrow corset of member states' constitutional law traditions (Harlow, 2002a:172). The EU framework is based on a dual legitimacy which "brings together states and peoples via a unique form of political integration",[24] in a process of governance "without government" organised around a single institutional framework.[25] The European Union constitutes a new legal order of international law the subjects of which comprise not only member states but also their nationals.[26] This legal order is based on two cornerstones: the direct applicability of Union law and its primacy over national law. This means, for example, that national administrative authorities should refrain from applying national provisions having direct effect that conflict with EU law.[27]

The institutional balance is ensured by a decision-making triangle made up of the Council, the European Parliament and the European Commission, where "[e]ach institution shall act within the limits of the powers conferred on it in the Treaties (...)."[28] The Treaty of Lisbon has further enhanced this 'trinomial' system, where effective cooperation between the institutions is the key element for success of the Union's objectives. Such system is based on the setting of the general political directions and priorities by the European Council,[29] with the joint exercise of legislative and budgetary functions by the European Parliament and the Council, on the basis of the Commission's proposals;[30] and on the latter's action as the 'executive' of the Union.[31]

The Council represents national governments, which are "democratically accountable either to their national Parliaments, or to their citizens".[32] It shall, jointly with the European Parliament, exercise legislative and budgetary functions" and "carry out policy-making and coordinating functions".[33]

The Treaty of Lisbon provides that "[t]he functioning of the Union shall be founded on representative democracy" and that Parliament is the institutional place where "[c]itizens are directly represented at Union level".[34] It "shall, jointly with the Council, exercise legislative and budgetary functions" as well as "functions of political control and consultation".[35]

Finally, the Commission "shall promote the general interest of the Union",[36] on the basis of its three-fold role. While member states have the main duty to ensure the application of Union law, as 'guardian' of the

Treaties the Commission has the authority and the responsibility to oversee member states' application of EU law and ensure its effective application.[37] Secondly, the Commission shall execute the budget and manage programmes, exercise coordinating, executive and management functions.[38] Not least, the Commission has the monopoly of legislative initiative.[39]

The Commission derives its political legitimacy from both the European Council and the European Parliament and it is made responsible to the latter.[40] Its members are "chosen on the ground of their general competence and European commitment from persons whose independence is beyond doubt".[41] Indeed, the cornerstone of the Commission's legitimacy is the independence from national and partisan interests.[42]

The Commission is not the EU's government[43] but a *sui generis* collegial body, with no match elsewhere. It deals with governments and institutions, rather than directly with citizens. It has evolved towards a specific model departing from the classical definition of *administration de mission* as opposed to an *administration de gestion*.[44] The Commission is a combination of both concepts: the scope of its competences is clearly delineated and most of its tasks have a technical nature. It lacks executive resources and, like for the EU budget, implementation tasks are mostly delegated to other structures (above all to national bodies). At the same time the Commission has the characteristics of an *administration de gestion* (day-to-day policy management, undefined life span, hierarchical and bureaucratic, represents the general interest) (Schön-Quinlivan, 2006:3-5).

Concluding remarks

Accountability is an 'umbrella' concept that encompasses different instruments (supervision and control, legislation, defined objectives and performance targets, codes of conduct of public officials). Adequate accountability processes require in particular a credible review of both expectations and results and an explanation of shortcomings and lessons learned. While effective accountability is not without cost, ineffective accountability can cost even more in waste, misuse of power and loss of the government's legitimacy in the eyes of the governed.[45]

Accountability is not just an 'icon' of modern public management; it is a critical condition for public authorities. Concerning the EU multi-level governance system it requires in particular giving account on the exercise of competencies conferred upon it by member states in view of reaching a better result than it would have been possible by the national level alone.

2. THE EU BUDGET: MANY HANDS, MANY EYES

As a consequence of the European Union's unique framework, EU public finances represent a kind of 'rare bird' in all aspects, from approval of the EU budget and its financing, through the management of its revenue and expenditure, until holding to account for its implementation.[46]

The EU budget intervenes in a increasing number of policy areas, and its effects are deployed practically everywhere in the world. Its implementation reflects the EU's multi-level governance based on the decision-making triangle made up of the Council, the Parliament and the Commission. As EU actions are guided by the subsidiarity/proportionality principles, roles and responsibilities are shared between the EU and national levels.

Why an EU budget?

As observed by the President of the European Commission, "[t]he European Union has many different tools in its toolbox. There is legislation. There is political cooperation. There is the persuasive power of 27 member states coming together with a common purpose. And there is the EU budget".[47]

Yet, what can the EU budget do that member states cannot do for themselves? Does the European Union's role in a given policy area necessarily require EU spending? Is more than €120 billion worth EU budget needed?

There is no straightforward answer to these questions. According to the criteria of need-for-action (or subsidiarity principle), a policy is financed by the EU for the very reason that (and only insofar as) there is an added-value as compared with funding from the national budgets. This means that one euro spent at the EU level can offer more than one euro at national level.[48] Therefore, the EU budget should do things that nobody else can (or will) do with better results. It represents an additional instrument in the constellation of EU public finances instruments whose main stars are the national budgets.

There are no 'objective' criteria for deciding whether a policy fulfils the conditions for EU financing, an issue largely debated in the academic world.[49] In fact, because of the integration between the European states, "nearly all policies have a European dimension and a national dimension".[50]

The decision to complement EU actions with spending measures is finally taken on 'political' grounds. In given situations, on the basis of different arguments, member states may decide that the 'European' level is preferable to the national one.[51] There could be various reasons:

- For agricultural policy, the objective was to create an integrated production area supported by a policy of common prices that could guarantee an adequate income for the agricultural community, to stabilise markets and to ensure the EU's own food supply at reasonable prices. Following the Common Agricultural Policy (CAP) reform in 2003, the CAP is today justified mainly in the name of environmental protection and rural development support. Aid is no longer strictly linked to production and it has the characteristic of a social solidarity scheme subsidising farmers' revenue.[52]
- Cohesion policy is clearly an exercise in solidarity, complementing national actions and integrating into them Union's priorities. The aim is to facilitate economic integration among member states, in particular after the accession of the states of Central and Eastern Europe.[53] The clearest reflection of this principle is additionality.[54] At the same time it is a 'Trojan horse' to improve and modernise public administrations, to enhance transparency and to foster good governance.[55] Similar observations may be made concerning the European Agricultural Fund for Rural Development (EAFRD) and the European Fisheries Fund (EFF).
- EU-funded research activities, the third main spending area, are meant to encourage researchers to cooperate across national boundaries and to share complementary skills and knowledge, thus generating in particular a 'behavioural additionality' favouring

higher quality and excellence in research. It has two main strategic objectives: to strengthen the scientific and technological base of European industry and to encourage its international competitiveness, while promoting research that supports EU policies.

- As for aid to non-member countries, EU financial assistance is a form of solidarity, namely concerning the economic and development assistance to developing countries. In some cases this is finalised to facilitate institutional reforms and to put in place adequate infrastructure (e.g. for candidate countries for EU membership).

The EU budget's financial size is also an issue for debate. In particular, it is often observed that the EU budget is too small as it corresponds to 'only' slightly more than 1% of member states' combined gross domestic product (GDP), while for example the federal budget of the United States of America represents the equivalent of some 20% of US GDP and that of Canada, some 18%. Comparisons are also made with the member states' budgets, which take up an average of around half of national income. A key reference in this context is the MacDougal report suggesting, more than 30 years ago, that in order to have a perceptible macroeconomic effect on the EU economy as a whole, the minimum volume of the EU budget should be 2 to 2.5% of member states' combined GDP.[56]

Such comparisons should however take account of the fact that today's EU budget does not in general finance goods and services aimed directly at EU citizens.[57] Its main role is to contribute to existing national policies, for example by providing funds for infrastructure and favouring productive investments, training, research and studies.

There is actually no 'ideal' or 'normal' size for the EU budget as such. Whether or not the EU budget is too small is basically a question that is only relevant once the objectives to meet have been set. As the Commission has said, "[t]he Union needs to ensure that its institutions continue to act effectively, that its policies meet their goals, and that its budget is commensurate with its objectives and with its financial resources."[58]

Revenue and Expenditure: Two sides of the same coin

The essence of the EU budget is largely predetermined by a multi-annual 'financial framework', whose aim is to "ensure that Union expenditure develops in an orderly manner and within the limits of its own resources".[59] This refers to the concept of 'budgetary discipline', whereby

EU spending must respect pre-determined ceilings as a brake to control growth of expenditure. See Box 2 for an overview of the EU's financial frameworks dating back to 1988.

Box 2. An overview of the EU's financial frameworks

The practice of adopting a multi-annual financial framework started in 1988. Four financial frameworks have been adopted: the Delors I (1988-92) and Delors II (1993-99) packages, Agenda 2000 (2000-06) and the current 2007-13 package (Inter-institutional Agreement of 17 May 2006). The financial framework determines the ceilings for commitments and payments in line with the ceiling on EU revenue. Amounts of expenditure in terms of appropriations for commitments should be established for each of the years and for each heading or subheading. Overall annual totals of expenditure should be also established in terms of both appropriations for commitments and appropriations for payments. Each of the absolute amounts set out in the financial framework represents an annual ceiling of expenditure under the EU budget.

The current financial framework sets the global level of payment appropriations to €820.6 billion (2004 prices), equal to 1.00% of EU gross national income (GNI). This amount, although significant in absolute terms, represents a relatively low share of public spending (member states' budgets as a whole account for almost 50% of the GNI). The financial framework, which was actually not foreseen in either the Treaty or EU legislation, used to be set by an Inter-institutional Agreement between the institutions involved in the budgetary cycle (the European Parliament, Council and Commission). It has now been incorporated into the Treaty on the functioning of the European Union (Art. 312 TFEU). It has to be adopted by the Council unanimously in accordance with a special legislative procedure (although the possibility exists for the European Council to authorise its adoption by a qualified majority), on a proposal from the Commission, and after obtaining the consent of the European Parliament. This means a right of approval and no genuine power of co-decision (although Parliament had previously no control on the multi-annual financial framework). The Treaty provides the possibility to reduce the present financial framework's duration from seven to five years in response to the Parliament's request to align future parliamentary terms with the Commission's terms of office. In view of its enhanced budgetary powers, the Parliament wanted to avoid being bound by a financial framework negotiated and adopted during the previous parliamentary term.

> The Commission has recently proposed to set the duration of the financial framework to 10 years, with a substantial mid-term review ('5+5'). This proposal is seen as an opportunity for a major re-prioritisation, leaving open for re-assessment the distribution of resources within headings, and the prioritisation within programmes and instruments (see COM (2010) 700, 19.10.2010, p. 23).

The financial framework is part of a global package where both revenue and expenditure are considered "complementary and inseparable".[60] It goes hand-in-hand with an agreement setting the burden-sharing among member states.[61] Any change to the multi-annual financial framework in fact requires re-opening an intergovernmental negotiation.[62]

As the European Union does not enjoy a financial autonomy to fix (and to manage) its financial resources, member states decide the amount to be put at the disposal of the EU budget as well as the type of resources. EU revenue is mostly provided through national contributions funded out of general taxation in the member states.[63]

Driven by the so-called 'budgetary balances',[64] which represent the accounting illustration that what is revenue for the EU represents expenditure for the member states, the EU financing system "has evolved piecemeal into a confusing and opaque mix of contributions and rebates",[65] in a complex arrangement of financial deals on a country-by-country basis. The European Parliament has observed that the nature of EU resources and the derogation regimes progressively added have made the revenue system "more complex, more opaque for citizens and increasingly less equitable and have led to a financing system which has resulted in unacceptable inequalities between member states".[66]

Indeed, as shown by the following figure, there is not necessarily a correlation between member states' GNI, meant to represent national income and therefore member states' contributive capacity, and their share in the EU budget financing. Whereas per capita contributions of well-off member states are generally above EU average,[67] the picture is quite different when comparing countries' overall contribution as a percent of their GNI. One may notice in this case that a number of countries contribute above their GNI share (Cyprus, Slovakia, Malta, Slovenia, Bulgaria, Portugal and Greece), while it is the contrary for other member states (the Netherlands, Ireland, the United Kingdom and Sweden).

Figure 2. Contribution to EU budget as a % of GNI and per capita (€) Deviation from EU average (2009)

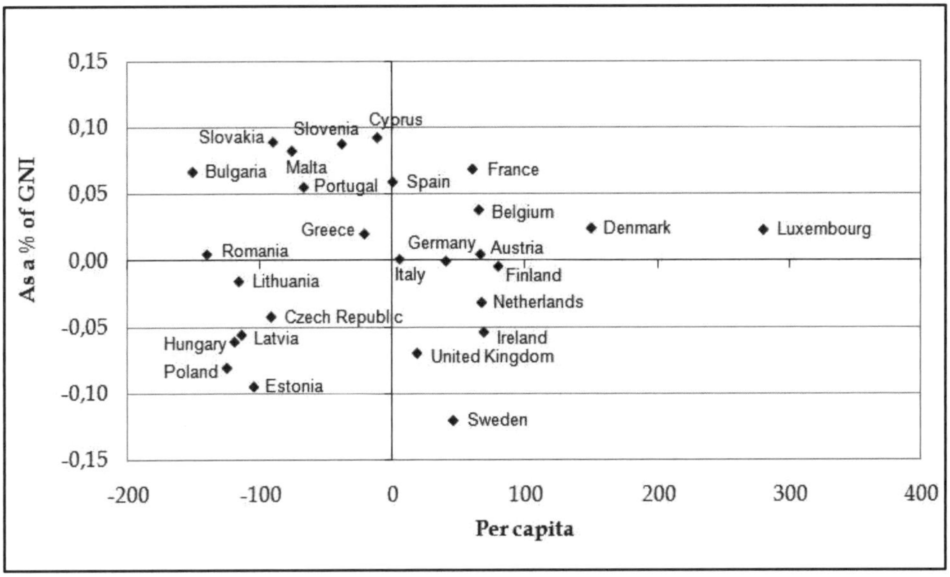

Sources: European Commission, 2009 budget and annual accounts and Eurostat figures.

Since EU revenue is not perceivable as such to taxpayers, they are therefore generally unaware about their individual contribution to the EU budget. Thus, as observed by the Commission, comprehension and monitoring of the present system on the part of citizens is virtually absent.[68] In this respect, the Commission's proposal (2004) for a genuine fiscal VAT resource reaffirmed the aim of achieving greater accountability on the part of the policy actors to the budgetary authority by giving taxpayers/voters a clearer view of the cost of Europe.[69] This would be in line with the oft-expressed desire to bring Europe closer to its citizens, so that in accordance with the principle of subsidiarity decisions are taken "as openly as possible and as closely as possible to the citizen".[70]

Decentralisation of power to local governments is a factor that may favour accountability (Seabright, 1996:85, 86). However, a major separation of spending and taxing decisions leads to lack of accountability in the public sector (Shah, 2004:38). Accountability may be said to be better secured when the funding scheme rests on a well-identified tax resource, insofar as debates in the decision-making bodies will then clearly be conducted in terms of effective tax-prices for the various categories of taxpayers, rather than in terms of national net benefits or costs (Begg et al., 2008:53). Also when (for example, Cohesion policy) mobilisation of EU funds requires national co-financing, local levels, not being responsible for raising taxes to finance the EU budget, will have less incentive to ensure that their spending is efficient. In particular, there is a risk that projects will be put forward mainly because funds are made available, on the assumption that 'spending' is a sufficient condition for achieving growth. As Parliament has observed, granting of funding "does not guarantee per se that it will be put to good use".[71]

It still remains that the idea of an EU tax, directly perceived on citizens, has never found member states' support; a position confirmed recently in the context of the Budget review.[72] If there are 'European' citizens, the taxpayers are still 'national'. There is one single taxpayer, EU and member states compete for the same revenues.

The opposition to the introduction of an EU tax directly perceived on citizens is justified on two main argumentations.[73] The first is that the allocation of genuine fiscal resources to the EU budget, in place of the present national contributions, is perceived as an unnecessary luxury. After all, financing the EU budget through national contributions has the advantage to provide the agreed resources without major difficulties. A second line of argumentation is that an EU tax would create hostility on the part of the public and would end up decreasing its support for the process of European integration.

The fear of provoking negative public reactions, however, is tantamount to admitting that the policies financed from the EU budget do not produce sufficiently convincing results about their added value. But then the public's support for the European cause can only be acquired by financing policies that result in identifiable achievements to the advantage of the European citizen. This is a precondition for both the acceptance of the corresponding taxation and the legitimacy of the EU budget itself.

Also, as the Commission's proposal for a VAT resource demonstrates, an EU taxation would not imply in itself increasing overall taxation.[74] But it would have the advantage of reducing the scope for arguments of the 'fair return' kind, which are the logical consequence of a revenue system based on national contributions.

The true argument against an EU taxation seems rather to be the fear that a genuine EU tax would open the door to a loss of national sovereignty, a pill that national chancelleries find hard to swallow. The key issue in this regard seems to be how (and by whom) the call rate of this EU tax would finally be set and whether the EU institutions will have a direct power of control over the taxable persons.[75]

Concerning EU expenditure, the multi-annual financial framework sets, in a rather inflexible way, the spheres of activity of EU finances and the amounts devoted to each spending area.[76] Most resources are pre-allocated on a country basis.[77] The EU budget, which must remain within the annual upper spending limits established by the financial framework, represents in its essence a seventh portion of it.[78]

Box 3. The EU budget process under the Treaty of Lisbon

The Treaty on the Functioning of the European Union has formally established subordination of the EU budget to the multi-annual financial framework (see Art. 312(1) TFEU). The process of adoption of the budget starts with the establishment, by the Commission, of a draft budget, i.e. an overall estimate of revenue and expenditure for the year ahead. This document is subsequently submitted to different stages of approval by the 'budgetary authorities', the Council of Ministers and the European Parliament. With the entering into force of the Treaty of Lisbon, the power-sharing between the Council and the European Parliament has been re-balanced and both institutions are put on an equal footing (see Art. 314 TFEU). Parliament and Council now have to reach a decision together on all of the budget. The new procedure, implemented for the first time for the 2011 financial year, provides for only a single reading of the draft budget by each institution. Both the Council and the European Parliament could reject the draft budget in the course of the procedure. A Conciliation Committee, composed of representatives of the Council and of the European Parliament, can be convened with a view to reconciling the positions and reaching agreement on a joint text. Once a joint text is agreed upon by the Conciliation Committee, the Council and the Parliament can approve or reject it. The Parliament may adopt the budget even if the Council rejects the joint text. In case both the Council and the Parliament reject the joint draft or fail to decide, the Commission has to submit a new draft budget.

The use of the appropriations is subject to adoption of a basic act, normally an act of the EU legislator.[79] EU expenditure generally takes the form of a reimbursement of inputs of 'eligible' national spending.[80] Although most of the EU funds (some 80%) are spent in agriculture and Cohesion policy, there are in total more than 70 spending programmes to which the EU contributes via various funds and financial instruments, covering a wide range of sectors.[81] These programmes normally contribute to similar programmes financed from national budgets.[82]

Many hands, many eyes

Under the EU's institutional power-sharing, it is the Commission that will "execute the budget and manage programmes", and this "on its own responsibility".[83] This competence is framed by a number of conditions. First, the Commission implements the budget "in cooperation with the Member States".[84] Second, this should be done in accordance with the Financial Regulation[85] (and other sectoral legislation), with the ultimate aim of ensuring compliance of EU spending with established rules. Third, the implementation should respect the ceilings set by the multi-annual financial framework. Finally, and not least, the budget must be implemented "having regard to the principles of sound financial management". And in this respect member states shall cooperate with the Commission.

The use of Union competences has a two-fold dimension: 'what' the EU should be doing, and 'how' this should be done.[86] In particular, the principle of proportionality requires EU interventions to be proportionate in all aspects to the objectives that can be better achieved at EU level, thus to be restricted to what is unavoidable to reach a given objective. As a result, EU spending programmes may be implemented through several management modes, which are very different in nature and imply a variable intensity of EU intervention. This concerns in particular the degree of decision by the Commission in granting the funds and its direct control at the level of the funds' beneficiaries.

Which management method applies to which policy is a matter for the EU legislative authority to decide upon; and it would be quite unusual for the Commission to oppose a stance backed by all member states. The Commission can implement the EU budget on a centralised basis.[87] Or, jointly with international organisations.[88] But more than 80% of the EU budget is managed in either 'shared' (mostly) or 'decentralised' management arrangements, i.e. through a multi-level governance involving national or third-country governments (at central and/or regional/local level).[89]

The implementation of the budget in 'shared-management' arrangements has three main characteristics:

- There is a two-tier system, a 'co-administration' based on partnership. Following delegation by the EU legislator, the Commission and member states are assigned different, although complementary, roles.[90] The financial implementation (Commission) is dissociated from the main decision-taking aspect (member states). Both delegated competences are put on an equal footing, i.e. there is no hierarchical primacy of the Commission over national bodies.[91] Also, the incumbency for the national level is a direct responsibility of member states themselves, not of their bodies. The setting-up of national management and control systems according to EU requirements as well as their operation is therefore in the end a member state internal issue.[92]
- Member states have primary responsibility for day-to-day management and control of EU expenditure. In particular, national bodies implement all the main management and control functions. They initiate and process the files for EU financial support; for example, they validate the claims of farmers entitled to receive EU agriculture support and enjoy broad discretion in selecting the beneficiaries and drawing up the programmes to be financed under the Cohesion policy. Also, national bodies execute the payments to the beneficiaries. In this respect, they must satisfy themselves that actions financed from the budget are actually carried out and ensure that they are implemented correctly.[93]
- The Commission's role consists essentially of putting in place the practical conditions for implementing measures the substance of which is predetermined by the multi-annual financial framework and the subsequent legislative acts adopted on that basis.[94] This means that the EU may well have a 'shared competence' in terms of policy, without necessarily having a corresponding competence in terms of its implementation.[95] For example, for Cohesion policy, the Commission is only informed of the largest projects proposed and it is not expected to micro-manage the implementation of the operational programmes. Therefore, due to the remoteness from the

field of the operations funded, the Commission commits and validates the appropriations without normally having a genuine control on the operations on the ground. This also explains why it is not in a position to know how effective national systems are in using EU money.

Box 4. Systems assessment

An assessment by the Commission of the strengths and weaknesses of individual member state's national systems for the administration and control of EU funds is a longstanding request by Parliament (most recently, see Resolution of 5 May 2010, with observations forming an integral part of its Decisions on discharge in respect of the implementation of the European Union general budget for the financial year 2008, Section III - Commission and executive agencies, point 135). One may notice that in the previous programming period (2000-06), in the event of 'shared management', and in accordance with the rules of sound financial management, the Commission was meant to first carry out document and on-the-spot checks into the existence, relevance and proper operation within the entities to which it entrusts implementation. This referred to the procedures applied, to control and accounting systems and to procurement and grant award procedures. The Commission had also the obligation to review such arrangements as necessary whenever there were substantial changes to procedures or systems in order to ensure continued compliance. This provision is no longer applicable since April 2007. Such basic *ex-ante* assurance is presently required in the sole case of indirect centralised management (delegation to executive agencies) and decentralised management (delegation to third country, national or international public-sector bodies).

Instead, as an implicit confirmation of member states' exclusive competence in putting in place the institutional arrangements for bodies in charge of implementing the EU budget, there are now far less ambitious measures limited to promoting best practices. Following a recent proposal of recasting the Financial Regulation, member states' systems would be exempted from an '*ex-ante* assessment' by the Commission, although sector-specific rules may provide for it a role in the accreditation process of national bodies (see COM (2010) 260, op. cit., Art. 53a(3) of the proposal, p. 73).

While under shared management arrangements, implementation is delegated by the basic legal act to both Commission and member states, decentralised management implies a delegation by the Commission to third countries whose administration is entrusted with implementation tasks (namely contracting). This management mode is based on an international agreement (often supplemented by memoranda of understanding) between the Commission and the third country concerned.[96]

The situation is rather different for other spending programmes, under the Commission's 'direct management'. For example for Research there are no fixed national or regional allocations. To bid for EU funds, potential beneficiaries respond to calls for project proposals (see Box 5 on research spending).[97] The Commission has therefore a direct contractual and control relationship to the beneficiary. Unlike in 'shared management', it performs in particular all the key control functions, where necessary engaging experts or contractors to carry out control or evaluation tasks on its behalf.

Being the 'executive' of the Union, the Commission's competences stem from a delegation by the EU legislator. Like in many countries, delegation from the legislator to an executive body of detailed rule-making and individual decision-taking is made subject to some form of supervision or control. This enables in particular the legislator to avoid excessively detailed basic acts, thus favouring flexibility and adapting to different realities on the ground.

In the EU context, a system for delegating implementing powers to the Commission has been in place since the 1960s. This system, known as 'comitology', consists of overseeing the exercise by the Commission of its implementing powers through the scrutiny of committees composed of member state representatives (the 'members' of a committee are the member states, not the individual persons) and chaired by the Commission. The idea was for member states to retain control over sovereign prerogatives transferred to the EU through their joint implementation.[98]

In practically all fields of EU intervention, committees must be consulted by the Commission on envisaged measures before it can adopt them. These measures may concern draft legislative acts, single decisions in specific cases or approval of EU funds in the framework of spending programmes. Committees apply different procedures (and voting rules). The choice depends on the content and scope of the implementing powers decided by the EU legislator in the basic legal act. An unfavourable opinion by the committee to a Commission's decision proposal means conditioning the decision-making to differing degrees, and can go as far as blocking the proposed measure. In practice, however, the Commission's proposals meet with a high level of consensus beforehand.[99]

The role of member states' representatives in the committees is understandably also to promote their country's expectations of getting a fair return in terms of funds allocation. This is why comitology has been criticised for representing *de facto* another way of transferring responsibility away from those who are supposed to be held accountable, being, at times, a forum for 'dividing up the spoils' of EU expenditure among member states.[100]

The Commission has pointed out in the past that the intervention of a management committee is likely to encroach on its exclusive responsibility as regards budgetary implementation and interferes at the same time with the European Parliament supervisory powers with respect to the implementation of the budget.[101] As a pre-condition for making the EU system more open and accountable to all European citizens, the Commission has considered that it should be "clearer who is responsible for policy execution".[102] It has thus advocated the down-grading of committees to an advisory role, the Commission thus remaining the body fully responsible for the decision on implementation measures, so that "[t]he Commission's responsibility for European-level implementation of decisions taken by the legislator would thus become clear and unambiguous for the people of Europe."[103]

The Treaty of Lisbon has retained a reference to mechanisms for control by member states of the Commission's exercise of implementing powers. Its entering into force will entail substantial modifications of the comitology procedures and would require the setting up of a new legal framework for the comitology system.[104] Also, the Treaty has extended the ordinary legislative procedure to most EU competences, thus making co-legislation between Council and Parliament the rule. Yet, if 'comitology' is meant to provide an opportunity for the EU legislator to be associated in the policy implementation, the present committees consist only of member states representatives. The European Parliament has no formal role in the process, though it is kept informed and can give its views. This opens a possible tension between the absence of Parliament from the committees and its increased role in the legislative process.

Box 5. Research spending, an example of the 'comitology' model

Research funding (over €50 billion for the 7th Framework Programme for Research, Technological Development and Demonstration activities for 2007-13) is based on a Multi-Annual Framework Programme, adopted by the European Parliament and the Council. The two institutions decide upon the overall allocation of funds and research objectives, the funding schemes and its instruments as well as the basic rules for running the research programmes (Rules for participation). Detailed funding and research themes are contained in *specific programmes* for research, adopted by the Council after consultation with the European Parliament. Finally, these programmes are further detailed into *work programmes*, adopted and implemented under the Commission's responsibility. Work programmes define in particular the funding schemes to be used, the content of the calls for proposals inviting candidates to submit a proposal as well as the evaluation and selection criteria to be applied to these proposals.

There are four programme committees under the 7th Framework Programme, one for each of the specific programmes. Programme committees, formed of member states' representatives, use most frequently the 'management procedure' and intervene at different stages. The Commission should obtain the Committee's agreement before adopting the work programmes. Then, at the issue of calls for proposals, the programme committee examines the list of projects approved by the Commission (normally in line with the experts' advice) and the list of projects rejected. The committee gives a formal opinion on funding of actions above a certain threshold. On this basis, a grant agreement is signed by the Commission. The Committee, which is regularly informed about the progress of each specific programme, is also consulted if the Commission wishes to change the indicative funding breakdown for the different specific programmes research themes.

The European Parliament is kept informed by the Commission of committee proceedings on a regular basis.

Concluding remarks

The size of the EU budget ought naturally to be determined by the sum of the costs of the various policies assigned to the EU. Whether a given policy requires EU spending (or non-budgetary measures only) depends on an assessment of its added value compared to national spending.

The volume of the EU budget is such that it seems no longer possible to avoid increasing awareness on the part of the public as to the cost of the policies funded. This is key to ensuring the necessary accountability of the management actors, compromised by the current opaqueness of the EU budget financing. As has been observed, an "examination of the funding of the Union is also part of the debate on the legitimacy of the Union's action".[105]

Although ultimately a responsibility of the Commission, implementation of the EU budget is the work of many 'hands' and many 'eyes'. The main management decisions are normally taken elsewhere than in Brussels. A plurality of actors, EU institutions but also (and not least) the 27 member states are involved in various forms. The Commission finds itself at the centre of a constellation of multiple and, eventually, conflicting interests. This presents the unique challenge for the Commission to promote the general interest as the 'executive' of the Union, on the basis of its three-fold role of 'guardian' of the Treaties, responsible agent for budget implementation and the holder of legislative initiative.

3. The EU Budget & Accountability

This chapter deals with the different dimensions of accountability for the EU budget (by whom and how, for what and to whom). It examines the scope of the Commission's 'ultimate' responsibility for the budgetary implementation and the different implications of the distinctive arrangements in place.

This refers in particular to 'shared management', which is the EU budget's main management mode, involving a high number of national bodies and a considerable remoteness from the EU funding source of the several millions of beneficiaries.[106]

Accountability: By whom and how?

As recalled earlier, the Treaty has entrusted the Commission with the ultimate responsibility for implementation of the EU budget, regardless of whichever entity is responsible for all or part of this implementation.[107] The extent of such responsibility is not lessened by the fact that the choice of the mode of the EU budget implementation is outside the Commission's remit (and it can therefore not repeal it), or that for a significant part of the EU budget there is a separation between financial implementation on the one hand and management functions on the other ('shared management'), with the involvement of member states' bodies.[108]

Indeed, management may be shared but the Commission's ultimate responsibility cannot, even with a national administration. As it recognised itself, "[w]hatever methods are used and whatever assurance mechanisms are pursued, there will always be an obligation on the Commission to ensure that control mechanisms are adequate to discharge its overall responsibility for the implementation of the budget".[109]

A complex control system

Due to its remoteness from the field, 'shared' management is undoubtedly the most challenging management mode for the Commission. Control of the implementation of these arrangements is a complex issue. As illustrated by the following figure, this is spread over several layers, involving not just EU institutions but also member states' implementing bodies and external audit institutions. This process is designed to provide to the Council and the European Parliament (EU budget authorities), but also to national parliaments, the basic elements for their oversight.

Figure 3. Overview of internal control and external audit of the EU budget ('shared management')

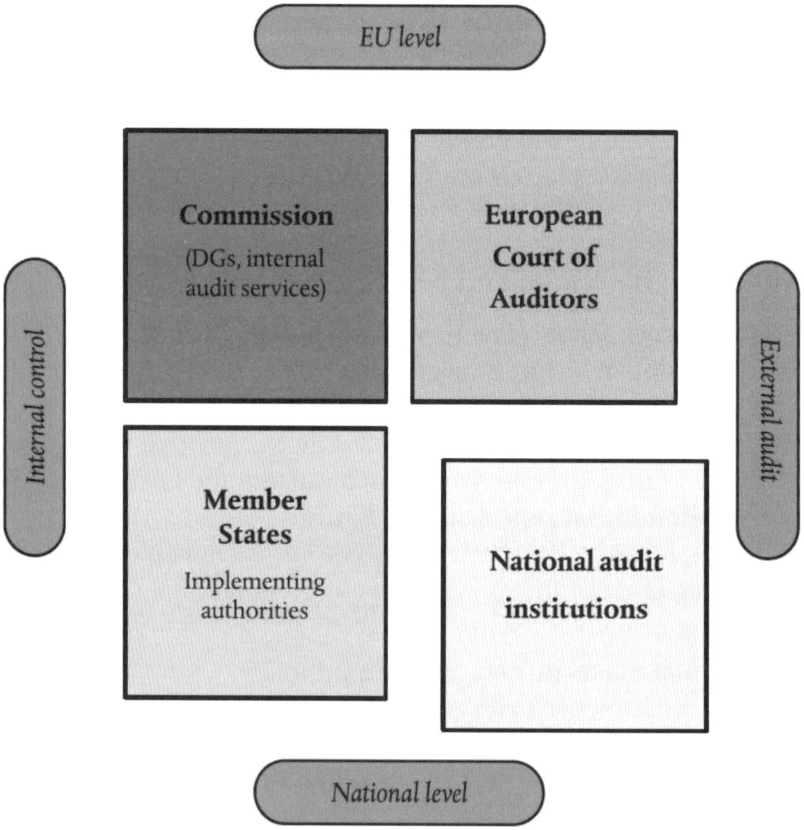

Source: European Court of Auditors, Opinion No. 2/2004 on the 'single audit' model.

As a translation into practice of the principles of partnership and common interest between all actors involved in 'shared management' arrangements, and to improve budgetary control mechanisms, Parliament put forward the concept of a 'single audit' chain of control procedures. The intention was to maximise the impact of controls on compliance of EU expenditure by streamlining member states' and Commission checks through their integration.

Box 6. The 'single audit'

The concept of 'single audit' has been promoted by the European Parliament, following concerns that "the control and audit activities in relation to the EU budget are characterised by a large number of auditors and audit services, each carrying out visits and drawing up reports almost independently but often on the basis of different standards". Parliament expressed the wish to examine "the feasibility of introducing a single audit model in relation to the EU budget in which each level of control builds on the preceding one, with a view to reducing the burden on the auditee and enhancing the quality of audit activities, but without undermining the independence of the audit bodies concerned" (see European Parliament resolution of 10 April 2002 containing the comments which form an integral part of the decision concerning discharge in respect of the implementation of the general budget of the European Union for the financial year 2000 (Commission), para. 48).

In its opinion on the 'single audit' model the Court of Auditors stressed that the EU internal control framework should be based around a logical chain structure where controls are undertaken, recorded and reported to a common standard, allowing reliance to be placed on them by all participants. Internal controls should provide reasonable assurance on the legality and regularity of transactions, and compliance with the principles of economy, efficiency and effectiveness. Controls should be coordinated to avoid unnecessary duplication. The 'owner' of the checks should be the European Union, not the individual control organisations (see European Court of Auditors, opinion No 2/2004 on the 'single audit' model (and a proposal for a Community internal control framework) - OJ C 107, 30.4.2004, p. 1).

It is no accident that Parliament's initiative followed closely the institutional crisis at the end of the 1990s, and the allegations of widespread mismanagement with a consequent lack of confidence in the Commission's ability to implement the EU budget properly.[110] Therefore, the implication that increased control requirements at all levels and tightened procedures were needed to restore public confidence in the management of the EU budget.

The underlying idea of the 'single audit' is a multi-level internal control framework, "integrated on the basis of clearly defined responsibilities for the various actors, established standards for the work required, and reporting systems and feedback mechanisms."[111]

The 'single audit' model has three main characteristics:

- There is one single control chain, starting from member states' bodies and ending up in the Commission. Mirroring the 'shared management' concept of partnership, each actor is supposed to rely on the previous one, so as to build up assurance at each stage and avoid unnecessary duplications and burden, in particular on beneficiaries. Subject to the effective functioning of the national control systems, the Commission can therefore abstain from controlling directly an infinity of beneficiaries with a corresponding immeasurable control effort.
- National bodies are primarily responsible for preventing, detecting and correcting ineligible expenditure. They represent a 'forefront' defence against irregular spending, based on an administrative structure set up according to EU rules. This provides in particular for an effective and efficient internal control system, a segregation of duties between different functions and an obligation for national bodies to inspect directly samples of expenditure claims and to recover irregular funding.[112] To mitigate the risk of failures in national systems and to ensure that they are operating as required, the Commission exercises a supervisory role over member states management and control systems. This is based on reporting by national bodies and on its own controls, including at beneficiary level.
- In line with the nature of EU spending, the system is fundamentally 'compliance'-oriented, as its aim is to secure conformity of EU spending with a set of rules defining the 'eligibility' of inputs of national spending (as opposed to disbursements based on a set of concrete objectives and linked to the achievement of results). The

focus is on the correct application of the financial, contractual and legislative rules.

The detail of controls and reporting functions at national level for Agriculture and Cohesion policy are reported in the Annex. One may notice the conceptual similarities of the two frameworks. Throughout the implementation period, the system entails far-reaching control and reporting obligations at national level about the management, monitoring and day-to-day financial control of the expenditure. There are three different control levels, independent of one another, and corresponding to three bodies operating on the basis of agreed control standards. There are, in particular, 'primary level controls' (to check compliance of final beneficiaries with their regulatory obligations) and 'secondary level controls' (checking the effectiveness of the primary level controls). Last, but not least, full compliance with established rules (European and national ones) of reimbursement claims presented to the Commission should be certified by a national body functionally independent of the spending agency. This is an essential element for the Commission to obtain assurance before proceeding to EU disbursements.

As an example, Figure 4 shows the assurance model for Cohesion policy, based on three building blocks, at both EU and national level, in the aim of preventing, detecting and correcting ineligible expenditure. The starting point is the set-up by member states, at the beginning of the programming period, of dedicated management and control systems. A pre-condition for EU disbursements is the Commission's assessment of their compliance with the required standards.

The Commission's supervisory function during implementation is based on an audit strategy over a period of years, building on the information provided by member states as mentioned in Figure 4. The intention is to principally rely on the work of the national audit authorities, in line with the single audit model. The Commission's role is also to provide guidance to member states and spread good practices among national bodies.

In case of failure of the 'forefront' line at member state level, the Commission has a number of means. Should its influence and persuasive powers not have the desired effect, there is the possibility to interrupt and/or suspend payments, up to cancellation of EU grants by disallowing the reimbursement of ineligible national expenditure.[113] In particular, at the end of the programming period, the Commission checks the closure declarations and carries out closure audits when it considers that insufficient assurance exists on management and control systems. In the Commission's own words, the *ex-post* clearance-of-accounts procedure at EU level represents the last line of defence to make good any loss to the EU budget, restoring a situation where 100% of EU expenditure is in line with the applicable rules.[114] In the end, the EU spending system as a whole is meant to be self-policing.

Figure 4. Control strategy for the Funds under shared management

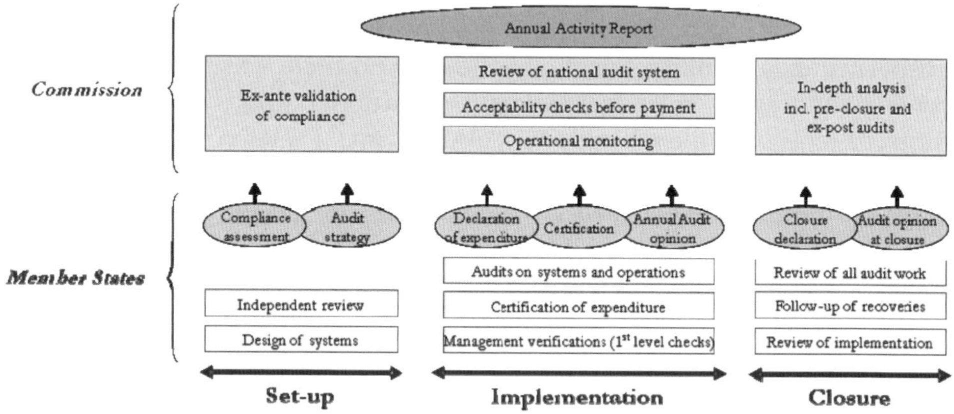

Source: European Commission, Annual Activity Report 2009 for Directorate-General Regional Policy, 31 March 2010.

It is a fact that the current multi-level assurance system does not as yet guarantee compliance of EU spending. The most obvious demonstration is given by the repetitive 'qualifications' of EU expenditure by the Court of Auditors.[115] Indeed, the Court's statement of assurance, a bill of health of EU spending compliance, shows year after year that not only is the 'forefront' line of defence at member state level not effective but also that the last line of defence at Commission level is 'permeable' and has not been able to prevent significant amounts to be paid out to member states on the basis of irregular national expenditure.[116] Although the Barroso I Commission made a strategic objective to obtain an unqualified statement of assurance from the Court by 2009, this objective was eventually not achieved.[117]

This is a matter for concern not just for the EU budget. A high irregularity rate in co-financed policies constitutes at the same time a warning signal for funds spent by the national budgets, either in the co-financing part or in similar projects totally funded by national funds.[118] The fact, for example, that a large part of the irregularities for Cohesion policies is attributable to infringements of procurement procedures reveals a failure to accomplish a long-standing objective of the EU internal market.[119] At the same time, this shows margins of improvement to ensure that EU activities are pursued at the best price.

The overall level of irregular EU payments shows a tendency towards reduction, but it remains high in significant areas of expenditure.[120] Although improvements are expected as a result of rules simplification and potentially enhanced systems introduced for the 2007-13 programming period, irregularities and related financial amounts reported by member states in 2009 have been increasing steadily for agriculture and Cohesion policy.[121]

If the idea of a 'single audit' system in 'shared management' arrangements is rather straightforward, its implementation proves to be far from an easy task. One of the main difficulties for applying one single system to a plurality of national bodies and to different spending typologies is to maintain comparable levels of application of rules. Therefore, the long chain of functions, duties and actors from member states to Brussels required legislating in great detail about who does what and how. As the Commission pointed out, "[t]he framework must be defined in sufficient detail to permit all participants in the control chain to identify and fully execute their role and to specify under which conditions assurances from the work of other management and control entities can be obtained".[122] Also, as EU spending is based on items of eligible spending, EU reimbursements were to be referred to a definite and commonly accepted legal standard: the 'eligibility rules', stemming from EU and national legislation.[123]

This EU 'regulatory zeal' was also meant to compensate for the Commission's remoteness from the ground field and its lack of legislative authority over national bodies, on the implicit assumption that the mutual trust between EU and the national level at the basis of 'shared management' should be sustained by a number of prescriptions and interdictions.

During the last ten years, systems' financial requirements and control procedures were repeatedly refined through successive legislative reforms. In turn, member states have often extended the scope of EU legislation by adding their own standards to EU requirements. This 'over-implementation' has resulted in a complex and tightly-woven set of legal and procedural requirements, increasingly felt as having developed towards a legislative labyrinth.[124]

Similarly to what economic theory suggests about tax burden, which becomes counterproductive beyond a certain point because excessively high tax rates discourage economic activity (and thus cause a decrease in tax revenues), too many legislative requirements may make the system ineffective. It is a source of potential misinterpretation, with a consequent high risk of rules-breaching above all by beneficiaries. This can therefore result in erroneous financial claims that need to be corrected, involving time-consuming procedures and end up in unnecessary administrative burdens at institutional and beneficiary levels. Also, over-legislation constitutes the humus for rule-obsessed bureaucracies and may thus deflect managers from content issues. Not least, it may deter potential applicants from seeking EU funds.[125]

A multiplicity of actors, over-legislation and over-auditing go hand-in-hand. The control system for EU spending, summarised by Figure 3, generates a significant number of controls (an 'audit explosion', Bachtler & Mendez, 2010),[126] with a consequent significant cost. The need of striking a reasonable balance between the administrative costs of control and the risk of reimbursing irregular expenditure has led to the concept of 'tolerable risk of error'. This is a recognition of how unrealistic it is to strive for a 'zero irregularity' system, due to the disproportionate cost of controls.

Box 7. The cost of controls

According to the Commission's estimates, the cost of controls for national bodies can account for 3% of yearly expenditure in entitlement-based schemes (like the payment of direct aids to farmers), up to more than the double (7%) for programmes, like Rural development, whose aim is to implement projects based on delivery of a defined output. This translates the fundamental differences between the two policies, the first based on the payment of an entitlement to farmers, the second on the implementation of projects aiming at improving the competitiveness of the agricultural and forestry sector, the environment and the countryside and the quality of life in rural areas and encouraging diversification of the rural economy. Reliable data are not yet available concerning the Cohesion policy, but given the similarities between the two policies, one may estimate that the cost of controls in this policy area should be proportionally as high as for Rural development.

At the Commission's level, the estimate is that at least 10% of the some 26,000 Commission staff is engaged in activities like financial management and accounting, internal control, anti-fraud, risk management and on-the-spot audits in member states and third countries.

One should also consider the cost for business entailed by administrative requirements and controls. According to a study undertaken at the request of the Commission, the total administrative costs/burdens for the Cohesion policy amount to more than €900 million. Most of this cost (almost two-thirds) is due to the obligation for final beneficiaries to submit information to the management authorities in order to draft the annual and/or final implementation report. Information obligations arising from the financial controls on the final beneficiaries on behalf of the member state authorities also give rise to a considerable share (14%) of the total administrative burdens (see Opinion of the High Level Group of Independent Stakeholders on Administrative Burdens, Cohesion policy http://ec.europa.eu/enterprise/policies/better-regulation/files/hlg_opinion_070709_cohesion_en.pdf).

As observed by the Court of Auditors in its opinion on the "single audit" model, any control system is a trade-off between the cost of operating the defined intensity of checks on the one hand, and the benefit these procedures bring on the other. The Court thus suggested setting the intensity of controls in the light of overall economic and political benefits. The Commission has recently proposed to insert in the Financial Regulation the notion of 'tolerable risk', to be decided by the Legislative Authority for each policy area, taking into account the costs of control, the risk or error and the benefits of the policy (see COM (2010) 260, op. cit., Art. 28b of the proposal, pp. 58-59).

While ten years ago the priority was to 'tighten the bolts', there is now a broad consensus that legislation may have gone too far and that there is a need for 'simplification'. This concerns not just the EU budget but EU legislation as a whole.[127] Indeed, simplification of rules may have the effect of reducing both administrative burdens and 'venial' irregularities. In this respect, a number of actions have been taken in recent times.[128] It remains, however, that simplification cannot be an end in itself and that there are limits to what one can expect from simplification measures in a multi-level system. Indeed, "a certain degree of complexity in rules and eligibility criteria is unavoidable as these are often fixed in order to achieve desired policy objectives, and are the outcome of a complex legislative procedure."[129] The more numerous are the actors, the more their roles and responsibilities need to be set by legislation, especially if they stem from different institutional contexts. An EU delivery system, based on a long chain of actors and items of eligible spending, cannot be a 'simplistic' one.

The need to strive for a 'sustainable' simplification, one that does not jeopardise the proper use of public funds, seems to be a recognised goal. For example, Parliament has recently asked the Commission to "continue its reflection on how to reshuffle the complex system of rules and requirements (...), without departing from the key principle of sound financial management".[130] The Council has drawn attention "to the necessity to maintain an appropriate balance between simplifying eligibility rules and targeting expenditure towards intended objectives, while not undermining the level of assurance provided by thorough controls."[131] The Court of Auditors has observed that "care is needed to ensure that due attention is also paid to the likely effects on the quality of spending of introducing simplification primarily aimed at reducing the level of irregularity."[132]

Diffused responsibilities

The tailoring of tasks between the EU and national level in 'shared management' has been the basis on which the Commission has long advocated an accountability framework in line with the equation 'shared management' = 'shared responsibilities', with two distinct lines of accountability, according to each party's management role. The intended aim of the Commission is to reduce its overall Treaty responsibility to its direct tasks, through the secondary legislation. This stance sounds like an implicit confirmation of the challenge of ensuring adequate implementation and enforcement of a policy delegated to other levels of government having a primary management responsibility. And in particular of the inherent difficulties to assess and endorse the considerable amount of information (reports, certifications) provided by national bodies.

Once again, the Commission is not the EU government, but rather a 'task-oriented administration'. In 'shared management', EU rules leave financial implementation mainly to the Commission and link its ultimate responsibility to the application of financially corrective mechanisms.[133] Thus the Commission tends to focus its attention (and therefore its account-giving) on the *ex-post* clearance against the benchmark of the eligibility rules.

Box 8. Sharing of responsibilities between the Commission and member states

Breaking down the responsibilities between Commission and member states in the EU budget implementation was part of a process initiated for agriculture spending and extended progressively to Cohesion policy, in particular since the 'Agenda 2000' reform package. The process has continued during the 2000-06 programming period, leading the Commission to progressively concentrate on programming strategy, compliance with EU policies, monitoring and control of implementation and evaluation of results, while national authorities assumed the responsibility for the implementation of the measures. Convinced that the provisions on accountability and sharing of responsibility with member states were not satisfactory, the Commission expressed the intention "to clarify with the Council its share of responsibility in meeting the objectives established for the shared management of the Structural Funds" as well as "to make proposals in order to align its monitoring and control powers to its responsibilities" (see European Commission, Synthesis of the Annual Activity Reports and declarations of the Directors-General and Heads of Service, COM (2002) 426, 24.7.2002, p. 10 and 30).

It is in this context that the Commission proposed to the European Convention, although unsuccessfully, to formalise in the Treaty the separation of responsibilities with the member states in "shared management" (see note 84). Along the same lines, one of the main goals of the regulatory instruments for Structural policies in the current 2007-13 programming period was meant to "clearly delimit…the framework, the nature, and the division of responsibility between the different actors concerned by the execution of the Community budget" (see European Commission, Proposal for a Council Regulation laying down general provisions on the European Regional Development Fund, the European Social Fund and the Cohesion Fund, COM(2004) 492, 14 July 2004, para. 5.3). The move towards increasingly transferring responsibilities to member states is confirmed by the Commission in its conclusions of the Budget review. The Commission envisages basing future EU reimbursements in 'shared management' on the declaration of payments by member states rather than on expenditure by beneficiaries (see COM (2010) 700, op. cit. p. 24). The key assumption, probably conditioned by the wish to obtain a "clean" statement of expenditure from the Court of Auditors, is the "de-coupling" of compliance of EU reimbursements to member states from legality and regularity of the expenditure on the ground.

Yet, if EU rules have passed to member states the substantive management decision power for which they have accepted primary responsibility, member states have not for all that accepted a dual accountability process making them directly accountable at EU level on the use of the funds they manage. Whenever this has been suggested, member states have opposed such a stance, even for policies where the EU budget supports the full cost of the spending programmes (e.g. payments to farmers). In this respect, national bodies' reporting and certification obligations represent nothing more than the fulfilment of a *conditio sine qua non* for EU reimbursements to take place. This reporting does not represent a disguised form of account-giving following the principal/agent concept.[134]

Member states tend to take the view that they only have control and reporting obligations towards the EU. As the Treaty says, governments are "democratically accountable either to their national Parliaments, or to their citizens".[135] So, they are not accountable at EU level, but neither are they often held accountable by their national parliaments for their shared responsibility for implementing the EU budget.[136] The key features of the system (financial agreement based on pre-agreed revenue and expenditure) tend to divest them of rendering an account. Absolved of collective responsibility, member states look the other way (Bachtler & Mendez, 2010:20).

The surge of 'dissecting' different functions has touched the Commission itself, leading to a further tailoring of responsibilities between Commissioners and their services. This is an outcome of the institutional crisis of the late 1990s and of the subsequent administrative reform. Since then Commissioners no longer perform tasks of budget implementation, like committing or paying expenditure or signing contracts.

As the Commission points out in the annual accounts, "[t]he College of Commissioners assumes collective political responsibility but in practice does not exercise itself the budget implementation powers vested in it. It delegates these tasks each year to individual civil servants accountable to the College and subject to the Financial Regulation and the Staff Regulations".[137] The concept is illustrated in Figure 5.

According to van Gerven (2007:2), 'political responsibility' could be defined as the possibility for a political organ to attach a political sanction to such misbehaviour on the part of a holder of public office, and/or to politically incorrect behaviour, such as failing to give complete information to Parliament, or giving incorrect or misleading information. van Gerven clarifies that a sanction for incorrect behaviour is characteristic of a parliamentarian form of government.

Figure 5. Responsibilities within the European Commission

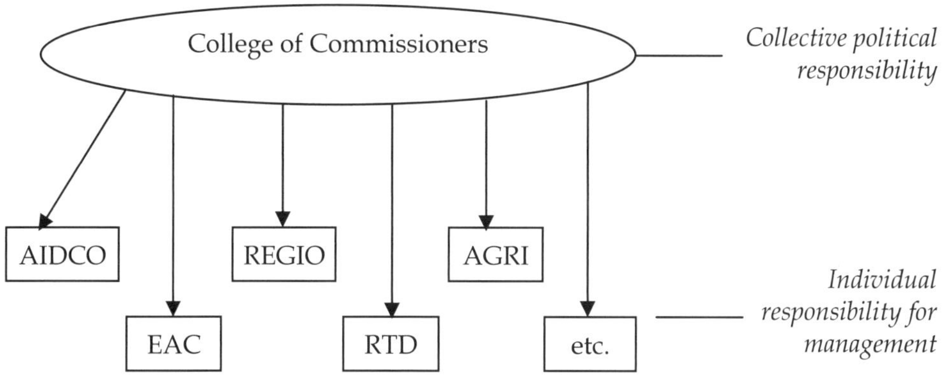

Source: European Commission (http://ec.europa.eu/budget/sound_fin_mgt/how_who_en.htm).

Concerning the College of Commissioners, political responsibility is a matter for the European Parliament before whom the Commission is responsible.[138] It starts with Parliament's approval of the appointment of the Commission President, as well as the College as a whole.[139] And it follows with the duty to give account in various forms to Parliament, normally through institutional reporting (in particular, Five-year strategic objectives, Annual policy strategy, Work programme, Synthesis of management achievements, Annual general report), answers to oral and written questions and evidence submitted to parliamentary committees.[140]

Concerning specifically the EU budget, the Commission submits annually the accounts to the budgetary authorities, the Council and the European Parliament. A recent addition (Treaty of Lisbon) is the obligation to establish "an evaluation report on the Union's finances based on the results achieved", in particular in relation to the indications given by the budgetary authorities.[141]

With reference to the EU budget implementation, the nature and the extent of the College of Commissioners' 'political responsibility' is a matter for interpretation.[142] Naturally, such responsibility cannot go beyond the institutional role given to the Commission. One should recall in this respect that the EU budget is based on two main 'political' decisions, both of which fall outside of the Commission's command. First, there is the multi-annual financial framework, which sets the map for EU spending and forms the basis for the subsequent approval of the annual budget by the European Parliament and the Council. Secondly, the adoption of the sectoral legislation and the choice of the implementation method. In the latter case, as in the case of 'shared management' arrangements, the main management decisions are reserved to member state bodies and "the Commission has to operate without full political authority whilst retaining under the Treaty full responsibility for the funds disbursed".[143]

As a result of the Commission's reform, Directors-General sit in the 'control room' of the EU budget implementation. They document their accountability to the College of Commissioners through their annual activity reports. In the Commission's own words, these are the pillars of its 'accountability architecture', whose apex is represented by the synthesis report, where the College sets out, for the attention of the budgetary authority, its conclusions on management achievements for each main spending area and on systemic cross-cutting issues. The College thus assumes "its political responsibility for management by its Directors-General and Heads of Service, on the basis of the assurances and reservations made by them in their annual activity reports".[144]

Yet, a number of factors limit the scope of the political responsibility endorsed by the College through the synthesis report, and hence its impact in terms of overall assurance and accountability.

The College's synthesis reports are based on presumed assurance, derived from the fact that "the European Union defines the necessary control mechanisms and the Directors-General concerned include in their annual activity reports a description of the control environment, and of the different tasks and responsibilities of all actors involved".[145] This may lead to the ambiguous situation, highlighted by the Council, whereby the Commission's synthesis report states that the control procedures put in place give the necessary guarantees concerning the legality and regularity of the underlying transactions, while acknowledging at the same time "that further efforts are needed to resolve a number of weaknesses".[146]

Before their finalisation annual activity reports are discussed between Commissioners and Directors-General. However, these reports are not endorsed by the College of Commissioners. This means that the College does not formally approve the management results and does not confirm compliance of the budgetary implementation with EU rules. Finally, like Directors-General's annual activity reports and in line with the Institution's role of 'task-oriented administration', synthesis reports focus on the executive functions and reflect the lack of power on the main management decisions.

Box 9. Directors-General' responsibilities

Initiated in the aftermath of the EU's crisis in the 1990s, the Commission's administrative reform was based on decentralisation of the management and control responsibilities at service level, to enhance Directors-General' responsibility for the matters entrusted to them. As a consequence, Directors-General are charged to ensure the entire management process, from determining what needs to be done to achieve the policy objectives set by the institution to managing the activities launched from both an operational and budgetary standpoint, including signing legal commitments, monitoring performance, making payments and, if necessary, recovering funds. The reform also introduced the obligation for each Director-General to present an Annual Activity Report and an Annual Declaration of Assurance. The report must indicate the results of the operations by reference to the objectives set, the risks associated with these operations, the use made of the resources provided and the efficiency and effectiveness of the internal control system. Directors-General must also arrange for evaluations to assess the viability of possible policy proposals, improve the decision-making process and increase the transparency, accountability and cost-effectiveness of EU intervention.

Moreover, they should also gauge the success and cost-effectiveness of programmes already underway (interim and *ex-post* evaluations). However, sectoral legislation may derogate to this principle and provide that evaluations are carried out by member states. This is the case for the Cohesion policy where ex-ante and on-going evaluation is a member state's responsibility and the Commission carries-out an *ex-post* evaluation (see Arts 47-49 of Regulation No 1083/2006, op. cit). Though without establishing a particular responsibility in the financial field as compared the ordinary provisions of the Staff Regulations, Directors-general may be held liable (including, subject to disciplinary proceedings, to pay compensation) in the event of serious negligence; in particular where the wrongdoing was made possible by inadequacies in the internal control systems devised and put in place under their responsibility.

However, Directors-general are not made responsible for management decisions taken by member states in case of 'shared management' policies. One may also note that due to the concentration of EU spending in few areas, most expenditure (around 80% in 2009) is implemented under the responsibility of four Directors-General (Agriculture and Rural Development; Regional Policy; Employment, Social Affairs and Equal Opportunities; and Research).

The absence of full insight into EU funds managed by member states has opened the door to criticism that the Commission assumes political responsibility "without knowing what happens with the funds in the Member States".[147] This is attributed by the Parliament to insufficient monitoring and supervision by the Commission, and to the absence of concrete solutions and accountability at member state level.[148]

Moreover, the distinction between 'political' and 'operational' responsibility within the Commission, between holders of public office and civil servants, has led to criticism of an implicit acknowledgment by the College that Directors-General implement the budget on their own, whilst their role is actually to perform duties following delegation from the institution.[149]

Concerns about a displacement of responsibility between Commissioners and officials as well as the fear that no one would ultimately take responsibility for the EU budget implementation go back to the institutional crisis at the end of the 1990s.[150] This led Parliament to suggest that the responsible Commissioner should co-sign the annual Declaration of Assurance given by the Directors-General, "as this would bridge the gap between the Director-General's individual assurance declarations and the College's institutional assurance declaration".[151] In this way the Parliament would get "an overall 'institutional' assurance statement to accompany the 'departmental' assurance statements which are what it gets under the current accountability structure."[152] The Commission claimed, however, that accepting the Parliament's suggestion "would call into question Directors'-General individual responsibility and blur the distinction between political (College) and management responsibilities/accountabilities (Director General)", leading *de facto* to an exoneration of Directors-General from any responsibility.[153]

As an example of the difficulties caused by diffused responsibilities and lack of ownership, the following box presents the case of the Galileo project. The project's management structure proved inadequate to cope with the needs. This prompted the Commission to put forward a different management structure, with the aim of strengthening public governance.

Box 10. The Galileo management structure

The Galileo programme is the last stage for establishing the European Global Navigation Satellite System (GNSS), the first worldwide satellite radio navigation and positioning infrastructure for civil purposes (e.g. vehicle navigation, commercial and safety services and services for government users).

The initial phases of the programme have been co-funded by the European Space Agency (ESA) and the Commission, taking responsibility respectively for the technological development and policy-making. The deployment and operational phase was due to be carried out by the private sector in the framework of a Public Private Partnership (PPP). However, in 2007, the concession contract negotiations failed as the risks involved were considered too high by the private consortium.

This failure provided the opportunity to redirect the Galileo programme. As a result, the programme will be financed and handled entirely by the EU under a strengthened governance scheme. Indeed, as observed by the European Court of Auditors, the previous programme's governance was inadequate. The division of roles between the different entities involved (EU and ESA member states, the Commission, Galileo Joint Undertaking and the ESA) was not clearly defined. There was no programme manager. This resulted in unclear lines of responsibility and many decisions were affected by the lack of a taker for full responsibility (see Special Report No 7/2009 on the management of the Galileo programme's development and validation phase, available at http://eca.europa.eu/portal/pls/portal/docs/1/2760294.PDF).

The change in the governance is shown by the following scheme.

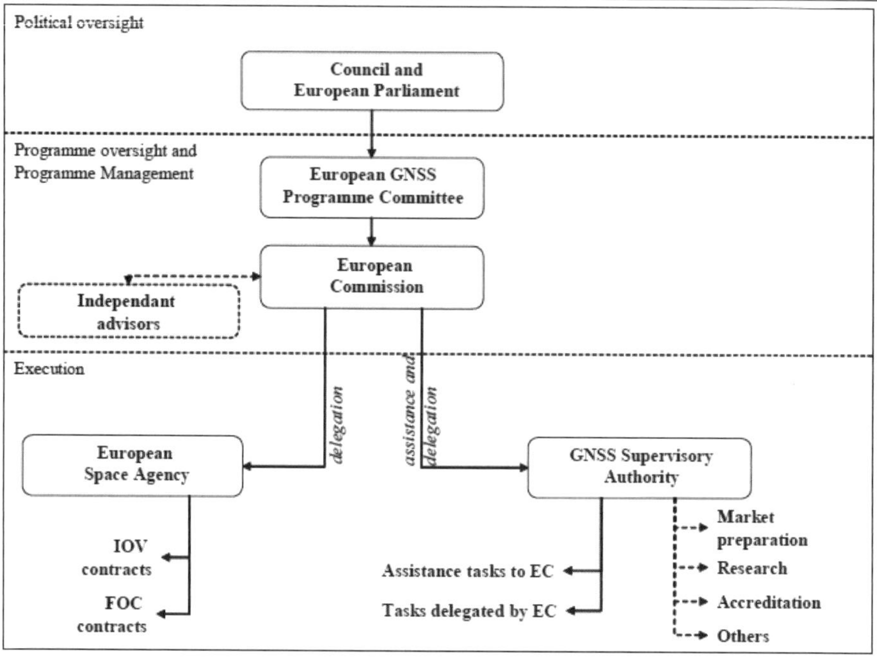

Source: European Commission, Progressing Galileo: Re-profiling the European GNSS programmes, COM(2007) 534 final, 19.9.2007

The governance scheme foresees a two-fold oversight. *Political oversight* belongs to Council and Parliament while *programme oversight* takes the form of a European GNSS Programme Committee, composed of member states' representatives. Overall programme management responsibility rests on the Commission which, as Programme Manager, is accountable for the entire Galileo programme. This has implied for the Commission to adapt its management capacity, both in house and with the support of qualified external advisors. The GNSS supervisory authority has the task to facilitate the introduction onto the commercial market of the services offered. ESA is responsible for the technical aspects of the project and is entrusted with the tasks of procurement agent. It acts on the basis of a detailed delegation agreement. It should also be mentioned that a Galileo Inter-institutional Panel, composed of representatives of Parliament, Council and Commission, has been set up in view of facilitating their close cooperation. The Panel will follow all relevant aspects, including the effectiveness of the governance arrangements.

The 'gap' in the process of holding to account for EU spending and the difficulty of reconciling one 'single' responsibility with a sharing of roles between EU and national level has appeared above all to Parliament as a major difficulty. Pressure was put in particular by repetitive qualifications of EU expenditure by the Court of Auditors, provoking growing concerns at both national and EU institutions' level for the loss of credibility for the whole EU spending system. Achieving a 'clean' statement on EU spending has therefore been a recognised political imperative since the early 2000.

Parliament took the view that, due to member states' important role in budgetary implementation, a 'clean' statement on EU spending could not be ensured by the Commission alone, the latter claiming that if the EU Court of Auditors cannot give positive assurance on the whole budget, this is because "[m]ost of the errors found by the Court concerned EU funds under national management".[154] Parliament's main concern was in particular that despite a number of statements and documents presented in a series by the Commission, there seemed to be no clear way out. Very often the debate took the appearance of a shuttling back and forward of individual responsibilities between Commission and member states, with eventually suggestions of further legislative and control measures, rather than viable and sensible solutions.

In order to overcome this 'standstill', the European Parliament proposed that member states should be involved at the highest level and that, therefore, the relevant political authorities should "take full responsibility for the funds placed at their disposal".[155]

Box 11. National management declarations

The European Parliament proposed that each member state should provide annually an *ex-ante* disclosure statement and an *ex-post* statement of assurance as regards its use of EU funding. The idea was that each member state's highest political and managing authority (Finance Minister), by signing an *ex-ante* Disclosure Statement and an annual *ex-post* Declaration of Assurance as regards the legality and regularity of national expenditure submitted to EU reimbursement, should formally endorse overall responsibility for the quality of the control and supervision at national level. The *ex-ante* disclosure statement was meant to confirm that the organisational structures put in place by the member state comply with the requirements of EU legislation and are expected to be effective in managing the risk of fraud and error in underlying transactions.

In this respect, the annual Disclosure Statement should include:

a) a description of the control systems by the managing authority of a member state,

b) an assessment of the effectiveness of these control systems,

c) a remedial action plan if necessary, drawn up by the managing authority of the member state in consultation with the Commission; and

d) confirmation of the description by a national audit institution or another external auditor.

The *ex-post* Declaration of Assurance should take into account the multi-annual dimension of the accountability process and the multi-annual nature of most EU programmes while at the same time giving assurance that the control systems have worked effectively during the year in question.

The Commission further elaborated on the Parliament's proposal, suggesting that member states' responsibilities should be assumed according to a 'four-pillar' scheme also involving oversight and reporting by national external audit institutions – a stance endorsed shortly after by Parliament.[156]

Parliament's aim was to obtain a kind of 'national' Statement of Assurance, by reference to that of the Court which represents by its very nature a global statement for EU expenditure as a whole, undifferentiated at national level. The innovative element was not so much for the declaration itself as similar requirements had already been introduced in the sectoral legislation (see Annex), but rather for the level of its signature.

Yet, the main issue seems to be not 'who' will sign such a declaration, but on which basis it would have been established; a 'clean' assessment should also be a 'right' one. As the Court of Auditors has pointed out, "[a] declaration that systems are functioning as required by EU regulations may not in itself provide assurance about the legality and regularity of the transactions concerned".[157] However, the Parliament was "convinced that a finance minister will prefer to establish properly functioning supervisory systems and controls instead of running the risk of having to explain to his/her Parliament why the national purse has to repay substantial sums to the European Union".[158]

Member states did not favourably receive the Parliament's request for a high-level political Statement of Assurance, or its further suggestion to split the *ex-post* Declaration of Assurance among several authorities, according to their competencies for the different areas of intervention.[159] In this respect, the Council of Ministers invoked the need "not to put into question the existing balance between the Commission and the member states or to compromise responsibility and accountability at the operational level".[160] Also, national external audit institutions were generally not prepared to be involved following the Commission's suggestion.[161] Nevertheless, some member states accepted, on a voluntary basis, to issue statements on EU expenditure managed by their own bodies.[162]

Some progress was achieved with the approval of the financial framework 2007-13. Member states accepted that "[a]s part of their enhanced responsibilities for Structural Funds and in accordance with national constitutional requirements, the relevant audit authorities in Member States will produce an assessment concerning the compliance of management and control systems with the regulations of the Community".[163] This should however be considered as a compromise at the lowest level. In the end, these summaries do not provide for an overall Assurance Statement, as they are just meant to summarise material existing in sector-specific reporting and declarations required for Agriculture and Cohesion policy. And despite the Parliament's request, the information provided by member states does not allow the Commission to assess in a reliable way "the strengths and weaknesses of each Member State's national system for the administration and control of EU funds".[164]

One might wonder whether this further requirement would achieve what the current 'cascade' of declarations at all levels in the spending process has not achieved. In particular, will this extra source of information help in making national systems more effective and less prone to irregularities? Announcing that a stock-taking exercise of the added-value of annual summaries is foreseen by the end of 2010, the Commission reached the conclusion that in order for the Annual Summaries to bring useful changes in shared management, a stronger legal basis is needed.[165]

The issue of national management declarations has become a political priority for Parliament that has also rallied support from national parliaments for holding national governments to account for their management of the spending of EU funds.[166] Parliament insists that these declarations should be "signed at an appropriate political level and certified by their national supreme audit body, as a means of administrative relief as well as improved administration of funds under shared management".[167] And it has requested the Commission to make the necessary proposals within the framework of the review of the Financial Regulation. Yet, the Commission's proposal of recasting the Financial Regulation does not seem to follow Parliament's request to place the holding to account for the EU budget implementation in 'shared management' at member states political level. Responsibilities are assigned to national implementing bodies, thus confirming the substance of current requirements in the secondary legislation.[168]

Divergent interests

The underlying assumption of the 'shared management' system is that, although they have different (but complementary) roles, the Commission and member states 'share' the same interests and pursue the same objectives. Indeed, "[p]ursuant to the principle of sincere cooperation", the EU and the member states shall assist each other in carrying out tasks which flow from the Treaties. Member states shall take any appropriate measure to ensure fulfilment of the obligations arising out of the Treaties and facilitate the achievement of the Union's tasks.[169]

It is however undeniable that the implementation of the EU budget brings substantial and direct interests into play for the member states. Indeed, the agreement on the multi-annual financial framework has both a revenue and expenditure side, the latter's geographical allocation being for a significant part already decided at that stage. EU expenditure represents at the same time the financial 'return' of national contributions paid to the EU budget.

At the beginning of the programming period, when it is about committing pre-allocated expenditure to member states and paying out pre-financing, the Commission and member states do not have many reasons for conflict. During and (above all) at the stage of the *ex-post* clearance (at the end of the programming period), Commission and member states start having potentially conflicting roles. This is in the logic of the system itself; member states defend tooth and nail what they consider their own prerogatives, above all their financial interests whenever the Commission threatens disallowing national expenditure. The former partners may thus become counterparts.[170]

For example, member states should make sure that their reimbursement claims are 'error-free' from the outset. This would ideally require an active form of oversight, with however the related costs for the controls and the subsequent risk of possible financial corrections by the Commission in connection with the irregularities uncovered. Yet, the immediate 'benefit' of disallowing national expenditure from EU reimbursement accrues to the EU budget, therefore resulting "in little incentive for Member States to devote sufficient resources to controlling EU funds".[171] Effective implementation of member states' control obligations is obviously influenced by the diversity of interests mentioned above.

The multi-level assurance system designed to ensure compliance of EU spending is only seemingly 'single'. In reality, it operates as a juxtaposition (and not necessarily as an integration) of two systems running in 'parallel', one in charge of financial implementation (Commission) and the other dealing with management functions (member states).

According to circumstances and the interests at stake, these systems may or may not pull in the same direction.[172] This also means that, contrary to the assumption made by the 'single audit' concept, the Commission's level of audit activity cannot be reduced significantly. As shown by the example in the box below, despite primacy of EU law, the requirement for member states to put in place adequate systems, ensuring that EU-funded operations are implemented correctly, may be overridden by other considerations.

Box 12. EU and national objectives may differ

Following a control, the Commission found serious weaknesses in the national management of a programme co-financed by Structural Funds to fight long-term unemployment and to facilitate the professional insertion of young persons and others excluded from the labour market (failure of monitoring by the responsible authorities over the beneficiaries, absence of supporting documents, lack of verification of the reality of co-financed actions and, not least, a certification not based on real costs).

As a consequence, the Commission had decided to withdraw €22 million out of €30 million initially allocated to the programme.

According to national law, this financial loss has been considered as a loss for the national budget itself. A legal proceeding against the official in charge of the implementation of the programme has been started. The national jurisdiction had established that EU funds were used for ineligible actions and that they had almost completely replaced national funds. The official has been given a fine of €5,000, in particular thanks to recognition of the following attenuating factors:

- management of EU funds was not a priority for the Ministry;
- there was a political consensus in the Ministry to use EU funds for ineligible actions to compensate reduction of national funds; and
- the internal control had approved all operations found to be irregular.

Source: Cour de discipline budgétaire et financière, Première section, Arrêt du 20 décembre 2007, Secrétariat d'État aux petites et moyennes entreprises, au commerce et à l'artisanat, Direction de l'artisanat, gestion des crédits du fonds social européen (FSE), N° 159-529), (http://www.ccomptes.fr/fr/CDBF/documents/ARR/Arret-159-529-ano.pdf).

The difficulty of putting national systems in line with requirements is shown by the development of the 'Contract of Confidence', an initiative launched by the Commission in 2002 as a way of implementing the 'single audit concept' in the Cohesion policy and reducing the administrative burden on member states due to EU controls. The idea of this voluntary commitment by member states was that subject to assurances on the proper functioning of national systems, the Commission would no longer carry out audits of the functioning of these systems for the programmes covered, nor of operations in such programmes, unless exceptional circumstances arise. For national systems to achieve this 'AAA rating' three conditions had to be met:

- the Commission had reasonable assurance that the systems complied with the requirements,
- the national authorities had drawn up a satisfactory audit strategy and
- the member state had provided an adequate basis for assessing the effective implementation of the audit strategy and set out conclusions with regard to the functioning of the systems.

As stated by the Commission, this initiative "has created a bench-marking procedure".[173] One would actually expect a normal occurrence that all systems are 'certified' as complying with the requirements of the 'Contract of Confidence'. Indeed, these requirements are nothing more than the logical consequence of applicable rules about 'shared management'.[174] However, this 'quality label' which could be defined as an indicator of voluntary compliance, has only been sought by few member states, for an amount representing less than 10% of Structural Funds (2000-06). This low popularity of the contract of confidence can only be interpreted as meaning that member states tend to play a rather 'minimalist' approach compared to what it is perceived as a more demanding standard.[175]

These examples confirm that the equation national interests = European interests cannot be taken for granted and that there could be instances where national and European objectives may diverge.[176] As has been observed, "[s]upranational systems of accountability are likely to confront specific challenges that arise from their location in a political space beyond states but one that rests on states" (Laffan, 2003:763). It is a fact that national bodies, which operate under the (national) authorities that have designated them and to whom only they are therefore accountable, "may be put in the position of the servant of two masters whose interests may differ very substantially" (Harlow, 2002a:184). The more so as they often combine purely national responsibilities with EU functions. National bodies are all naturally susceptible to 'local' pressure and sympathetic to (sometimes very short-term) national/local concerns, which may well outweigh 'EU' pressure. In case of conflicting priorities, the 'remoteness' factor, typical of the EU budget implementation, represents an objective element favouring the predominance of national interests.

Financial corrections: A shortcut for accountability

The Commission's supervision over national systems is mainly based on desk-reviews and a limited number of controls which cannot cover all funded actions. Due to the multi-annual nature of many spending programmes, such controls would often only take place on the basis of a multi-annual cycle during the programming period. As a result, assurance on conformity of expenditure is not ultimately sought annually but several years later, at the stage of the multi-annual *ex-post* clearance.[177] The view is taken that there is no urgency, that a greater risk of error in the interim claims can be accepted because of the possibility to apply financial corrective mechanisms later. After all, possible creditors being mostly the member states, there is no problem of 'solvency'.

Therefore, when the Commission's Directors-General declare (subject sometimes to reservations for member states' systems) "that the control procedures put in place give the necessary guarantees concerning the legality and regularity of the underlying transactions",[178] this should not be interpreted as a statement on the legality of EU spending for a given year. In practice, with their declaration Directors-General express confidence that systems will make sure, sooner or later through clearance procedures, that only expenditures that comply with EU and national rules will be subject to reimbursement by the EU budget.

One may refer in this connection to the distinction between 'police patrol' and 'fire alarm' approach, in the meaning of active and passive forms of oversight.[179] The advantage of 'police patrol' oversight is that the actor is under continuous and direct control, while in a 'fire alarm' framework there is less active and direct intervention.

Although for different reasons, the Commission and member states are inherently 'fire alarm' oriented. 'Police patrol' oversight implies a lot of resources and, above all, an integration of the different control activities within a common system. In this respect, as discussed earlier, the 'single audit' model, due to different interests at stake, has developed towards a 'juxtaposition' rather than an integration of the different control stages. Member states are tempted to await the outcome of the Commission's checks (and audits of the Court of Auditors) and react in consequence. To undertake such a 'police patrol' oversight on the basis of the Commission's own forces would be unthinkable. With several hundreds of national bodies involved, a proper scrutiny of systems operation by the Commission would require far more resources in its control departments than presently available.

There is therefore in the present context of a plurality of spending programmes and a significant number of financial actors no other alternative than a second-best solution, based on a fire-alarm scrutiny diffused among the EU and national level, reacting *ex-post* to individual warnings.

A first consequence is that assurance has to be presumed in the absence of evidence to the contrary. National systems continue to manage EU funds for years without an undisputed assurance that they fulfil the basic requirements, and that therefore the operations co-financed and the related spending are eligible for EU reimbursement.[180] While in 'shared management' arrangements compliance of EU spending is supposed to be based essentially on efforts from member states, as recalled earlier, they have no particular incentive in devoting significant resources to controlling EU funds that could end up in a cut of their EU spending share. Nor do they have an immediate interest in applying financial corrections for actions that they have approved and paid for in the first instance, and that, moreover, they may consider as a due counterpart of the financial framework agreement.

In the logic of a EU spending system conceived to be ultimately 'self-policing', if member states fail to correct irregularities, or if the Commission concludes that there are serious failings in the management and control systems that may give rise to systemic irregularities, then the Commission may impose financial corrections on the member states.[181] In fact, this possibility has become for the Commission an essential counterweight to member states' responsibilities in ensuring compliance of EU reimbursements, assuming that this instrument constitutes for them a deterrent to declare 'ineligible' expenditure.[182] *Ex-post* clearance has been transformed into a kind of 'gatekeeper', or in the Commission's words "an essential safety net at the end of the control cycle".[183] At the same time, as EU spending is based on eligible inputs, *ex-post* clearance marks out the borders of the 'eligibility' conditions for EU reimbursements and constitutes in practice the yardstick for compliance.[184] This is true to the point that one could actually argue that in its essence the Commission's ultimate responsibility for actions in 'shared management' represents more a task (the application of financial corrective mechanisms) than a true responsibility for the EU budget implementation as a whole.

The effectiveness of *ex-post* clearance in both 'cleaning' national expenditure and representing a deterrent against irregularities does not meet with unanimous agreement.[185] The question is in particular whether financial corrective mechanisms are sufficiently dissuasive, comprehensive and fully repairing the damage to the EU budget.

A first consideration to be made is that financial correction mechanisms do not constitute a penalty system.[186] *Ex-post* clearance is limited to counteract 'ineligible' spending (in whatever way this could have been estimated), and does not take account for example of recidivism or other aggravating factors. In line with the principle of proportionality, financial corrections constitute a simple recovery of undue payments from the member states, i.e. the result from the difference between member states' declared expenditure and expenditure recognised as eligible by the Commission and chargeable to the EU budget.[187]

The Commission's aim is limited to shielding the EU budget from ineligible expenditure paid out to member states. Hence *ex-post* clearance only targets them; it represents no more than an accounting correction, whose scope is not to rectify erroneous payments at the root.[188] Whether, as required by EU rules, *ex-post* clearance represents a first step of a recovery process of undue payments from the final beneficiaries is left in practice to member states. Indeed, the Commission's view is that according to the principle of shared management, recovering irregular payments to beneficiaries "is the sole responsibility of Member States".[189]

When the Commission implements the budget directly (for example, Research spending), single beneficiaries may have to reimburse part or all expenditure received as a result of a financial correction.[190] By contrast, the final beneficiary of EU funds in 'shared management' arrangements may feel in the end no impact whatsoever as these corrections are mostly supported by member states themselves, an issue about which Parliament has expressed concern.[191] A first reason is that, as shown by the example in Box 12, national bodies may themselves be at the source of the irregularity. Also, the recovery from beneficiaries is problematic when a financial correction is established on a flat-rate basis, in the absence of a valid link between the irregularities and the amounts to be recovered.[192] A further reason is when financial corrections become 'socially' relevant and risk attracting protests, for example, from a professional category.[193]

The fact that financial corrections by the Commission for agriculture and Cohesion policy (some €2.9 billion in 2009) are usually borne by member states has two further main implications. The first is that this turns into an extra cost for national budgets and therefore into a disguised additional 'tax', which is at odds with the aim of pooling national resources at EU level in view of allowing member states "to cut their costs, avoid overlaps and get a better return on their investment".[194] The second consequence is that a transfer of 'ineligible' expenditure from one public budget to another is simply to sweep the 'dust under the carpet'. The irregularity remains and 'ineligible' expenditure continues to be supported by public funding.

Also, the establishment of financial corrections does not necessarily mean that EU funds are recovered by the Commission and that member states' financial allocation is reduced correspondingly. To avoid this, member states tend to over-declare national expenditure in order to create a buffer of eligible items, as in the case of Cohesion policy where EU spending represents often a limited fraction of national spending. In this field a financial correction generally represents (for some 70% from 2000-09) a simple substitution of new projects for 'non-compliant' ones.[195]

Recovery procedures entail administrative costs, at the level of both the Commission and the member states and take a long time before they materialise.[196] When financial corrections result in a net reduction of a member state's financial allocation, they are likely to lead to legal disputes and often generate long drawn-out procedures whose outcome is uncertain. With the consequence, noted by Parliament, that "the systematic imposition of sanctions on Member States has resulted in a reluctance by Member States to disclose implementation problems".[197]

Further, it is difficult to know whether such corrections provide a comprehensive estimate of all undue payments.[198] The argument often used that subsequent checks conducted throughout the whole programme's duration would have corrected the irregularities may be appealing, but it is not convincing.[199] The Court of Auditors has observed that there is, at present, insufficient information available to support this claim.[200] And, as the Commission admits, there may still be a 'residual risk' several years after the end of the programming period.[201] Also, one cannot rely on member states to spontaneously make the necessary corrections in full. Available data show that irregularities detected by individual member states may be far below the amounts ultimately documented by the Commission.[202] This gives a concrete indication of the diversity of interests, mentioned earlier, between member states and the Commission. It also shows that the amount of financial corrections depends to a significant degree on the number of controls that the Commission (and the Court of Auditors) may perform during the time-scale period allowed.[203]

By their very nature, financial corrections are much more appropriate for violations of specific compliance rules rather than weaknesses in terms of sound financial management, namely lack of results. For example, the extent to which expected outputs, outcomes and impacts are achieved by EU programmes is not the basis on which a financial correction is triggered. Although compliance with eligibility rules is a key condition for effective spending, it is only one side of the coin.

As they often come at the end of the programming period, there is a risk of not seeing the forest for the trees. Financial corrections tend to correct for specific uncovered irregularities. They may at most limit the damage for the EU budget by recovering, years after, the funds spent, but it is unlikely that they may resolve systemic problems. If systems have not operated in line with the requirements, it is no longer possible to correct *ex-post* fundamental weaknesses and it is too late to 'close the barn door' and cause a deterrent effect on other claimants. As has been observed: "[t]he (…) disadvantage of *ex-post* control increases with the time lapse between the date on which expenditure is made and that on which it is queried".[204]

The question of the supposed crucial effect of financial corrections should be raised: do the birds return to their nest after the shot? The regular (and increasing) occurrence of financial corrections has made them seem an inevitable routine procedure, thus demonstrating the limited deterrence of this instrument and its reduced effectiveness in causing structural repairing effects.[205] One might therefore question to what extent, as argued by the Commission, financial corrections represent "a strong incentive for the Member States to improve their management and control systems and thus to prevent or detect and recover irregular payments to final beneficiaries." [206]

As a matter of principle, one should however not welcome a situation where a significant amount of EU payments has to be reimbursed because of irregularities. Indeed, financial corrections are above all an indicator of whether a policy has been implemented according to established rules. The higher the amount of financial corrections, the higher the evidence of failure and missed opportunities. As observed by the Council about Cohesion policy, the final objective should not be "to increase the amount of corrections but to maximise the correct use of the funds".[207]

Accountability: For what?

By reference to the treaties and secondary legislation, there are three different levels of requirement for the budget implementation under 'shared management' arrangements, representing as a whole the 'standards' for EU spending. First, the Commission is required to implement the budget "having regard to the principles of sound financial management", a responsibility that implies cooperation with the member states.[208] A second level of requirement is represented by the essential minimum standards that member states' management and control systems involved in EU spending must meet.[209] A third level concerns the nature of expenditure that can be reimbursed and under which conditions – the so-called 'eligibility rules', which are complemented by national rules.[210]

As a result of its ultimate responsibility in implementing the EU budget, one would expect the Commission to give account on all three levels of requirement. Indeed, 'compliance' and 'performance' is not an 'either/or' option between quantity and quality; assurance should exist on both.[211] While compliance refers to different standards than 'value for money' criteria, it is a fundamental condition for achieving a proper use of public funds; "[t]he EU added-value concept is not only about doing the right things. It is also about doing them right."[212]

Box 13. Sound financial management

As early as the EEC Treaty of 1957, auditing the budget had been entrusted to an Audit Board with the purpose of establishing that "the financial management has been sound" (Art. 206 TEC). This mandate was confirmed in 1975, when the European Court of Auditors was created. It was much later that 'value for money' was elevated to the rank of institutional principle for the budget implementation (1992, Maastricht Treaty). A few words were added to Art. 205 TEC (then 274 TEC and nowdays Art. 317 TFEU) to indicate that the Commission shall implement the budget "having regard to the principles of sound financial management". The Treaty of Amsterdam (1997) further amended Art. 274 TEC by providing that "Member States shall cooperate with the Commission to ensure that the appropriations are used in accordance with the principles of sound financial management".

In 2002, a thorough reform of the Financial Regulation further clarified the scope of the concept of 'value for money'. In particular, the obligation was introduced to set "specific, measurable, achievable, relevant and timed objectives" for all sectors of activity covered by the budget. The Regulation also stated that compliance of EU spending with the principles of economy, efficiency and effectiveness should be checked by means of performance indicators established per activity and measurable in such a way that results can be assessed (see 11th Whereas and Art. 27(3) of the Financial Regulation, Council Regulation (EC, Euratom) No 1605/2002, op. cit.).

One should note that the concept of 'value for money' has not yet found a clear understanding in practice. For example, concerning Cohesion policy, EU rules provide that the managing authority shall be responsible for managing and implementing the operational programme in accordance with the principle of sound financial management. Yet, its tasks are basically related to compliance requirements (see Art. 60 of Regulation No. 1083/2006, op. cit.). A similar ambiguity is contained in other institutional texts. Thus, in the section on "Sound financial management of EU funds", the Inter-institutional Agreement on the 2007-13 Financial Framework indicates the importance of strengthening internal control, giving priority "to sound financial management aiming at a positive Statement of Assurance, for funds under shared management." (see the Inter-institutional Agreement of 17 May 2006 between the European Parliament, the Council and the Commission on budgetary discipline and sound financial management, op. cit., paragraph 44).

This text refers however to the annual Statement of Assurance by the European Court of Auditors, a statement about compliance of EU revenue and expenditure, not 'value for money'. Similarly, the Commission's report on the functioning of the Inter-institutional Agreement on budgetary discipline and sound financial management (COM (2010) 185, 27.4.2010) contains a section "Sound financial management of EU funds" which actually only refer to compliance issues and financial resources available. Not differently, the Commission's proposal for a draft Inter-Institutional Agreement between the European Parliament, the Council and the Commission on cooperation in budgetary matters (COM (2010) 73, 3.3.2010) contains a similar section which does not in fact deal with 'value for money' issues.

The Commission's Directors-General are meant to take responsibility "for implementing revenue and expenditure in accordance with the principles of sound financial management and for ensuring that the requirements of legality and regularity are complied with".[213] Among other things, their annual activity reports "shall indicate the results of the operations by reference to the objectives set" as well as "the use made of the resources provided".[214] Yet, the scope of Directors-General responsibility has to be put into the context of the executive functions devoted to the Commission. Thus, their annual activity reports focus on funds disbursement, an assessment of member states' management and control systems on the basis of the available information and compliance of spending with the eligibility rules.

Whether the policy objectives set have been achieved and whether the expected outcomes have been produced remain outside the scope of Directors-General responsibilities, as these results depend on a broader set of circumstances that are beyond their control.[215] This is particularly the case in 'shared management' arrangements where the Commission knows generally very little about the day-to-day implementation of EU-funded actions. As recalled earlier, it has practically no say on the main management decisions, those that (like the identification of beneficiaries or the selection of projects) determine (or undermine) 'value for money' spending. Hence, Directors-General are not expected to take responsibility for any failure for policies on which they only have an indirect impact.

Therefore, when Directors-General declare that they have reasonable assurance that the resources assigned "have been used for their intended purpose and in accordance with the principles of sound financial management",[216] this should be understood as restricted to the executive activities under their own direct responsibility. The word 'resources' does not refer to the funds managed in the framework of a given policy, but rather concerns the use by the directorate-general of available means (above all, staff) in respect of financial management procedural requirements (namely, issuing financing decisions, executing payments and clearing accounts). Similarly, in the declaration that information contained in the annual activity reports "gives a true and fair view",[217] the devil is in the detail; a footnote explains that this means "a reliable, complete and correct picture of the state of affairs in the department".[218]

With the 2010 draft budget, the Commission has presented for the first time a 'Budget Memorandum', meant to provide "an overview of the main achievements which have been or will be delivered by the EU budget."[219] The intention is to highlight concrete achievements as a consequence of EU funding, "in particular in relation to their impact on business activity, employment creation and economic growth".[220] Organised around the four priority areas of the Lisbon Strategy (people, business, infrastructure and energy, and research and innovation), the purpose of the 'Budget Memorandum' is to link "the budget proposal to objectives and delivered results such as 'creation of new jobs' which is essential for EU citizens and businesses during the economic crisis".[221]

Yet, as do Directors-General Annual Activity reports, the Budget Memorandum takes shelter by stating: "The depicted results are achievements or estimations based on available information in activity statements and it cannot be guaranteed by the Commission that the target will be met." It also indicates that for some indicators "external factors will also have substantial impact on the final results" and that for "some policy areas such as Regional Policy the list of deliveries only include information for those Member States who provided the relevant information in their operational programmes".[222]

Concerning member states, their obligation to cooperate with the Commission to ensure 'value for money' cannot be more than a general principle as long as it is not spelled out into a practical and meaningful procedure of account-giving. Yet, accountability cannot be effectively imposed if the criteria against which conduct is to be measured in the process of calling to account are not made clear.[223] As recalled earlier, the information provided by member states is finalised to fulfil a requirement to obtain the EU reimbursement, it does not embody a true accountability process.

If 'value for money' aspects remain in the dark in the accountability process for EU spending, this is also due to a number of structural factors. A main difficulty is to distinguish the effects of EU measures from all the others. EU policies' main aim is often to 'support' similar programmes financed from national budgets, to provide 'the icing rather than the cake'. These programmes represent a relatively marginal financial contribution to far-higher funded national policies.[224] Moreover, there has been a tendency over the years to increase the number of spending programmes. There are more than 70 of them, covering a wide range of policies.[225]

As shown by the table below, only eleven programmes have been granted funding of more than €1 billion per year. These programmes absorb 94% of available appropriations, the lion's share being taken by Agriculture and Cohesion spending. None of them belongs under the heading "Freedom, Security and Justice" or "Citizenship". One should add, concerning the remaining 6% of funds, that this is divided-up among 65 spending programmes, two-third of which have been endowed with no more than €100 million per year. Actually, funding for 30 of these programmes is between €1 and €30 million per year.[226] There is therefore an issue of critical mass that permits the showing of tangible results.

Table 1. Current EU spending programmes ≥ €1 billion/year (current prices in millions of €)

Heading	Programmes	Total amount	Average/year	% over Total
2	Market expenditure and direct aids	301,579	43,083	33.2
1b	Structural Funds	278,256	39,751	30.7
2	Rural Development	96,444	13,778	10.6
1b	Cohesion Fund	70,110	10,016	7.7
1a	Seventh Framework Programme for research, technological development and demonstration activities	50,554	7,222	5.6
4	Development Cooperation Instrument (DCI)	17,298	2,471	1.9
1a	Community financial assistance to projects in the field of energy (EERP)	3,980	1,990	0.4
4	European Neighbourhood and Partnership Instrument (ENPI)	12,356	1,765	1.4
4	Instrument for Pre-Accession Assistance (IPA)	11,622	1,660	1.3
1a	Nuclear research and training activities	4,001	1,178	0.4
1a	Trans-European transport network (TEN-T)	8,038	1,148	0.9
	Sub-Total	854,238	124,062	94
	Total (Headings 1a-1b-2-3a-3b-4)	907,829	132,204	100

Source: Author's elaboration from "Financial programming 2011 - 2013", SEC(2010)473.

Legend:
Heading 1a – Competitiveness for growth and employment
Heading 1b – Cohesion for growth and employment
Heading 2 – Preservation and management of natural resources
Heading 3a – Freedom, Security and Justice
Heading 3b – Citizenship
Heading 4 – European Union as a global player

At the same time, EU spending programmes often have 'all-inclusive' objectives. As observed by the Court, these are too wide-ranging, unclear or somewhat conflicting; policy instruments and resources are insufficient to meet the objectives set; causal links between the funded activities and the desired outcomes are unclear; and there are deficiencies in monitoring and evaluation arrangements.[227] The scope of Cohesion policy is a clear example of this.[228] Although operational programmes should contain quantified targets and a limited number of indicators for output and results, to make it possible to measure the progress in relation to the baseline situation and the achievement of the targets, in practice the link from an intervention's inputs to the production of its outputs is very limited. This makes it even more difficult to establish the subsequent link to impacts on society in terms of outcomes.[229] The lack of selective and focused objectives is directly reflected in the difficulty in setting measurable indicators for the policies financed. This in turn undermines the role of the *ex-post* evaluation and the potential 'pedagogical' effects for future policies.

Another factor that affects giving an account for 'value for money' is that the EU system is based on inputs of 'eligible' spending items; conditionality for EU reimbursements is not based on achievement of pre-agreed outputs, outcomes and impacts.[230] This is the reflection of a financial framework inspired by 'fair return' considerations whose clearest illustration is the geographical pre-allocation of funds.

There are also policies whose intrinsic nature makes the 'value for money' element extremely difficult to assess. For example, since financial aid and agricultural production were separated, financial support for agricultural markets is very close to granting a financial entitlement (like a pension right) to farmers on the basis of the physical situation of the individuals concerned (area farmed), albeit in exchange for certain requirements concerning environmental protection.

If member states produce some overall information on targets and expected results (although not subject to an external quality assessment as to the reliability of the performance information), this does not go as far as requiring them to link the broad policies objectives with specific outputs, outcomes and impacts. In this respect, the *ex-post* Evaluation of Cohesion Policy Programmes 2000-06 shows that although quantitative targets were often set and an indicator system established, in many cases they were not linked in a meaningful way to ultimate policy objectives and determined in relation to the funding made available and what it could plausibly achieve. Accordingly, targets were either attained far too easily or were unattainable given the funds deployed.[231] In many member states the main focus tended to be on processes and financial implementation rather than on the actual results of the programmes and the effectiveness of the projects supported. Monitoring and evaluation systems were often not integrated into the decision-making process.[232] The risk is to turn evaluations into a requirement rather than an opportunity, hence making evaluations very much an issue for 'experts' rather than for politicians to draw lessons from.

A number of reports and evaluations provide indications on overall expectations and achievements, for example in terms of GDP growth or impact on employment.[233] But it is one thing to argue that EU spending has (or will) contribute to produce some defined results; it is another to answer the question whether these funds were used in the most effective way. And to further demonstrate that compared to national spending, EU funding has resulted in a better added value, which constitutes in the end the *raison d'être* of the EU budget.

As the Court has observed, "[i]nsufficient information on results and outcomes also undermines accountability and transparency as well as decisions on the allocation of resources".[234] For example, while stressing in general that "the focus actually given to the legality and regularity of the spending does not help to inform the legislator and the public as to whether the money has been spent effectively",[235] Parliament has regretted the "lack of detailed information and comparative studies with rankings on the advancement of regions that profit from Structural Funds".[236]

As has been observed, "[t]he EU budget is a key tool for delivering the Union's policies, and the effectiveness of EU spending can therefore have an important influence on whether the EU matches the expectations of its citizens".[237] Yet, if EU rules provide an obligation for spending to comply with 'sound financial management', there is no framework for 'performance' accountability. In particular there is no specific accountability process giving account of member states' responsibilities for the main management decisions, those conditioning in the first place effectiveness of spending. The Commission recognises that it should be in a position to demonstrate that public funds are well targeted and well managed.[238] However, as a result of placing "the law at the service of what is possible rather than let it express the impossible"[239], 'value for money' remains outside the scope of its account giving.[240] It is therefore not possible to provide a conclusive answer concerning the use of funds and their impact, thus making all the more fragile the Commission's ultimate responsibility.

Accountability: To whom?

The final control of the EU budget implementation takes place each year before the budgetary authorities to whom the Commission submits the accounts of the previous financial year. It is for the European Parliament, acting on a recommendation from the Council, to give a discharge to the Commission for the budgetary implementation.[241] In this respect, Parliament has a general power "to hear the Commission give evidence with regard to the execution of expenditure or the operation of financial control systems" and to submit any necessary information.[242] It should also be mentioned that Parliament has the faculty to set up a temporary Committee of Inquiry to investigate alleged contraventions or maladministration in the implementation of EU law.[243]

The discharge procedure constitutes more than the formal act of closing the accounts and a certificate of good conduct releasing those responsible from any further liability in respect of the management of the budget. It is also the means for citizens to exercise, through Parliament's representation, their "right to ask a public official for an accounting of his administration".[244] The point for Parliament is in particular, to "identify the problems which lead to mismanagement and a deficit of financial control", to "ensure that the Commission takes the necessary steps to put a lasting end to the shortcomings and omissions established" and to make sure "that unduly paid or uncollected amounts are recovered".[245]

The discharge procedure also represents a political judgment on the way the Commission has discharged its ultimate responsibility. It "offers the political authorities an opportunity to assess the management of the financial resources of the European Union, to propose measures for its improvement and to express an overall political judgment on its quality".[246] In particular, the Commission is bound to take all appropriate steps to act on the observations of both the European Parliament and the Council concerning the implementation of the EU budget; and it has to report back on the measures taken in the light of these observations.

In case of dissatisfaction, Parliament may postpone the discharge decision or even refuse to grant discharge.

Box 14. Postponing and refusing to grant discharge to the Commission

The European Parliament may *postpone* the discharge decision (see Art. 145 of the Financial Regulation, op. cit.), namely to ask the Commission to provide further information or in order to impose on it certain conditions which must be fulfilled beforehand. Postponements were decided for the financial years 1990, 1991 and 1996 and, lastly, for the financial year 2007 for the section concerning the Council. The principle of *refusing* discharge is not provided for in the Treaty nor in the Financial Regulation. It derives from an interpretation given by the European Parliament to its own powers (see Arts 3 and 5 of Annex VI to Parliament's rules of procedure). A decision by Parliament to refuse the Commission a discharge because of serious objections must be considered exceptional. Discharge has been refused twice (instead, the accounts were only noted by Parliament) – in November 1984 in respect of the 1982 financial year and in December 1998 in respect of the 1996 financial year. In 1984, Parliament's refusal of discharge was motivated by a series of failures on the part of the Commission and the lack of adequate remedies proposed. The Thorn Commission did not resign only because its term of office was to expire a few weeks afterwards. In 1998 Parliament's refusal of discharge was provoked by a lack of transparency and the difficulty for the Commission to drawing the necessary consequences following cases of bad management within its services. The Santer Commission resigned in March 1999, under the threat of a censure motion, immediately after publication of the first report of the Committee of Independent Experts. More recently, Parliament has refused to grant discharge to the Director of the European Police College in respect of the implementation of the College's budget for the financial year 2008 for not meeting the standards of good administration set by the financial rules (see European Parliament resolution of 7.10.2010).

A decision by Parliament not to grant discharge for the implementation of the budget may have serious political and institutional consequences. This may lead to the extreme measure (however not automatic) of adopting a motion of censure intended to attach a political sanction to misbehaviour on the part of the College of Commissioners and leading to its resignation as a body.[247]

As observed by the European Court of Auditors, there is a close link between the Commission's ultimate responsibility for implementing the budget and the significance of the discharge procedure, in particular the effectiveness of the budgetary authorities' recommendations.[248] Yet, if following the Treaty, the discharge process is addressed towards the Commission as the ultimate responsible body, the latter feels uncomfortable in taking any commitment for actions under member states' responsibilities; and, understandably, even more to bear the blame for the policy management, which is a formal member state responsibility and about which it knows very little. The Commission tends therefore to return the ball to member states whenever questioned by Parliament about the management on the ground.

Giving the sharing of roles between the EU and national level, it is not surprising that Parliament considers the discharge procedure as part of a process seeking to establish full accountability not just on the part of the Commission but also from other actors like the member states' bodies.[249] However, Parliament does not have the authority to question national administrations regarding their management of EU funds. Actually, national bodies have no 'institutional' relationship with EU institutions, since member states are the statutory Commission's counterpart and bear in the end responsibility for actions undertaken by their bodies. But national ministers are not subject to EU parliamentary scrutiny. As discussed earlier, pressure on member states for more accountability has resulted in a limited outcome due to their reluctance to being held to account for their own management responsibilities.

With the discharge procedure, truth will out. As a result of the diffusion of responsibilities and of the lack of an overall master ship for the EU budget implementation, the accountability framework is only to a limited extent "a relationship between an actor and a forum, in which the actor has an obligation to explain and to justify his or her conduct, the forum can pose questions and pass judgment, and the actor may face consequences" (Bovens, 2006:9). The discharge procedure remains in the middle of the ford and resembles for the main management decisions a kind of 'trial' *in absentia* as Parliament lacks a responsive interlocutor. This is not without a sense of disappointment in what a significant expansion in the amount of auditing and evaluation undertaken for accountability purposes "is able to do to ensure that those responsible for government performance are held accountable for their actions" (Bemelmans-Videc & Lonsdale, 2007:15).

Further, a possible motion of censure against the Commission following Parliament's refusal of discharge would not change the fact that the Commission lacks legislative authority over national bodies. A new

Commission, whose appointment is in any event a shared competence with member states,[250] would not necessarily be more successful in ensuring better management on the ground. Also, more 'vigorous' action in promoting infringement procedures against member states might prove to be inimical to efficiency. And Parliament alone cannot decide the management mode for a given policy. EU spending compliance would still have to rely ultimately on clearance mechanisms, with the limitations discussed earlier.

There are therefore grounds for considering the effectiveness of the present discharge arrangements, especially taking into account that Parliament's faculty of giving discharge was decided more than thirty years ago on the grounds that due to a significant expansion of EU spending, "the implementation of the budget should be more closely supervised".[251] Parliament's dissatisfaction has recently prompted it to call for "a comprehensive debate on the current discharge procedure system" with EU institutions, member states, national parliaments and supreme audit institutions.[252]

4. THE ACCOUNTABILITY GAP

The EU budget is "one of the most significant tools to guarantee the accountability of the European Union towards its citizens (...); an accurate and accountable use of the EU resources is one of the essential means to reinforce the trust of the European citizens."[253] Indeed, democracy is ill-served "when the decision-making process is obscured by complexity, when those whom the citizens can sanction are not always those who take the decisions or are reluctant to shoulder their share of responsibility before the people who voted them in."[254] Among the principles of good governance one principle stands out, this is the accountability to ordinary citizens. Yet, it is a fact that the characteristics of the current EU finances framework are at the root of a number of 'side-effects' affecting the accountability to citizens (and taxpayers) for the use of EU funds. Three main difficulties should be noted.

As the EU budget is funded through governmental contributions, citizens are not directly aware of how, to whom and how much they pay for the EU budget. Not surprisingly, the EU budget remains a mystery to many Europeans.[255] In their daily lives, citizens may come across information about EU budget-funded initiatives, but unlike for national expenditure, nothing draws attention to the fact that a portion of their fiscal burden is actually used to fund EU expenditure. Yet, the volume of the EU budget is such that it seems no longer possible to avoid increasing European citizens' awareness about the cost of EU programmes. The famous 'no taxation without representation' principle is applied at EU level the other way round.[256] There is representation (namely through the European Parliament), but no visible and explicit taxation for the EU budget. Citizens are therefore not stimulated to demand a proper account-giving on the funds spent, and thus pressure from public opinion plays a limited role in influencing the decision makers. As observed by the Commission, while visibility to EU citizens has an important accountability dimension, their comprehension and monitoring of the present system is virtually absent. The lack of a direct relationship between citizen and budget is another manifestation of the 'democratic deficit'.[257]

A second difficulty is due to the nature of EU spending. EU disbursements are not made conditional upon achievement of specific outcomes and impacts, but are based on items of 'eligible' expenditure. Moreover, this is regulated by a complex legal framework whose consequence is a 'fear of error', often overwhelming policy considerations and best use of funds. There are no established procedures for rewarding best performers. Also, in a 'budgetary-balances' driven system, 'fair return' considerations invite member states to seek 'acceptable' net balances rather than specific policy objectives, leading to an inevitable trade-off between desired outcomes and spending levels. Absorption of funds also becomes an objective, and potentially an objective in itself when there is a risk of losing funds following de-commitment.

This situation encourages the dispersion of resources in a multitude of small initiatives whose main characteristic is to be easily put forward rather than their intrinsic added-value, introducing a tension with the aim to make efficient, effective and economic use of funding by pursuing specific policy objectives.[258] In many cases political objectives are not commensurate with the resources made available; there are funds, but not necessarily specific EU policy targets. Spending programmes are numerous and often entail grand, 'all-embracing' objectives. However, due to a combination of several factors (ceiling on EU revenue, strict allocation of resources to spending headings and concentration of resources for the most part on Agriculture and Cohesion policies), relatively limited funds are available for many programmes, and in most cases probably below the critical mass necessary to produce recognisable results. In those cases there is obviously a risk of EU funds being scattered in the 'ocean' of similar national actions, thus reducing not only the significance (and visibility) of EU interventions, but also affecting their potential effectiveness. The prevailing logic of doing 'something' with the available resources ends-up, *de facto*, in an exemption from choices of purpose. Whilst arousing high expectations, the objectives of EU spending programmes are not really "specific, measurable, achievable, relevant and timed" as they should be.[259] This hampers the possibility to monitor their achievement, and it makes it extremely difficult to identify (and report on) the added-value citizens get in return for their money - a potential source of scepticism and even hostility towards the EU.

Finally, 'shared management', the main management mode, does not necessarily rest on 'shared interests'; national bodies play at the same time a 'national' and a 'European' role. The objectives to be pursued on these two 'levels' may in practice be different and sometimes in conflict since EU spending is equally a form of national income. This tension has prevented putting in place a single and consistent multi-level management system under a Commission's effective supervision. Instead, inspired by the tailoring of tasks among actors set by the regulatory framework, several management structures are juxtaposed, often operating on separated rail tracks. The risk is a process of depersonalisation leading to proceduralism and formalism overtaking substance, leading as an unavoidable consequence to sub-optimal decisions. A system where more and more is being observed, quantified, verified and reported on, but in which increasingly less operational action is being taken.[260] The system is 'fire-alarm' oriented, basically 'sniffing for fires'. Risen to the keystone of a 'self-policing' EU spending system, *ex-post* clearance has become the yardstick for compliance, leaving aside 'value for money' concerns and thus giving a narrow interpretation of the requirements meant to be the standard for EU spending. The increased focus on the application of financial corrective mechanisms is actually a symptom of the inability to achieve the intended objectives. Moreover, their cost is generally supported by national budgets (and not by faulty beneficiaries), thus ending up in a 'socialisation' of losses and representing a further burden on taxpayers.

There is *de facto* no single 'owner' for EU spending. Each actor gives account to different authorities according to different requirements, standards and modalities; thus responsibilities for the budget implementation are (and remain) diffused. There are actually four different levels of responsibility intervening in the budget implementation. There is first the legislative authority (Council and Parliament) setting the design of spending programmes, the management mode and other conditions (like the rules for participation in research programmes). Then there is the executive, split for most of EU spending between the Commission and member states. And finally, there is a further sectioning within the Commission, due to the separation of the Commission's College responsibilities from those of its Directors-General.

There is an overall 'accountability gap'. While member states ensure the main management functions, the latter are not held to account at EU level for their duties.[261] Despite being ultimately responsible, the Commission only assumes a 'putative' fatherhood for the EU budget implementation. It tends to retain a rather formal responsibility for policy set-up and its operational implementation. The scope of this responsibility is basically limited to the function of financial management of the appropriations and the application of financial corrections, making thus of *ex-post* clearance a shortcut for accountability.

As has been pointed out, key to accountability in practice is how those responsible are held to account. When accountability is not working well, there is no reporting or inadequate reporting on performance; there is no serious, informed review of the information reported; and neither are there appropriate programme changes nor consequences for responsible individuals.[262] The various difficulties related to the EU budget implementation impact on the main requisites for effective accountability in shared governance arrangements. This points in particular to weaknesses about the setting of commonly agreed objectives, the clarity on the expected results and the partners' capability to meet expectations.

The knock-on effect of all this is that Parliament receives insufficient information, in particular fair and reliable performance information that would allow it to develop the demonstrated capacity to learn and adapt if things go wrong. In the absence of a responsive interlocutor, the discharge process before the European Parliament resembles for most of EU funds a 'trial *in absentia*'. And as a result, citizens are unclear about who is supposed to 'give account' and to be 'held to account' for what and to whom.

Yet, for institutional (but also practical) purposes, roles-sharing between the EU and national level in the EU budget implementation is necessary. However, member states do not seem prepared for constitutional reasons to give account at EU level. How can this circle be squared? It seems clear that a new concept for the EU budget must go hand-in-hand with appropriate institutional reform setting governance and administration of the budget by intentional action, i.e. well-defined EU objectives. Once again, the question is: 'Why Europe?'.

5. SQUARING THE CIRCLE

If we do nothing, fate will deal with our present difficulties, in spite of ourselves.

Jean Monnet

No one could reasonably believe that the fundamental shortcomings of the present EU budget could be solved with 'simple' and straightforward solutions. The decision-making mechanisms have not proven so far to be conducive to change, basically due to the absence of incentives to overcome the focus on 'fair returns' (Gros, 2008:2). Any change may potentially affect the delicate institutional balance of powers among the EU institutions, as well as between them and the member states well beyond any likely financial impact.

The problem is that "while everyone agrees in the abstract on the need for reform, as soon as the debate moves to concrete measures, there seems to be a strong bias in favour of the status quo".[263] If a test of the sensitivity of the matter (and of the vested interests at stake) is needed, it is sufficient to see the raft of criticism generated by a leaked initial draft of the Commission reform proposal.[264]

Indeed, there is always someone who can lose out from any reform. No change may appear to many as a merit in itself and a relatively 'safe' solution; the highest merit being that, contrary to change, one might believe that it does not require an explanation. However, a failure of the budget review process will not be devoid of consequences. Immobility and lack of demonstration of the EU budget's added-value could lead in the short/mid-term to its 'sterilisation' and its progressive 'disintegration' through various forms (re-nationalisation, *ad hoc* intergovernmental agreements in line with a Europe *à géométrie variable*).[265] The risk is that the EU budget will slide into irrelevance, paving the way to denying its *raison d'être*.

A few factors play potentially against a *déjà vu* scenario. As often, urgency is dictating the European agenda. The economic crisis has put the spotlight on member states' severe public deficits, requiring the adoption of rigorous measures to significantly curb public spending. It seems unlikely that for the EU budget things can go on 'as before', as if nothing happened and it could escape contributing to tougher budgetary discipline and rigour.

The economic crisis has also shown that the European Council has taken decisions on economic and financial matters and policies that would have seemed unrealistic only months before. Nothing prevents the same from happening to the EU budget as well. The more so as the European Council has considered the multi-annual financial framework 2007-13 as an overall negotiation package of which the budget review was one of the clauses.[266] This suggests that if the agreement on the current financial framework was in the end imposed by the timing, the call on the Commission "to undertake a full, wide-ranging review" covering all aspects of European Union spending and revenue[267] was more than a ritual statement. After having clearly claimed the need to implement significant changes in the EU budget delivery process and its key role in reinforcing the trust of the European citizens, member states have no true interest in a failure. Faced with such significant issues, it is for them a matter of credibility to agree on far-reaching reforms and not just purely 'cosmetic' changes on the basis of the lowest common denominator.

It is also worth recalling that the Treaty of Lisbon "marks a new stage in the process of creating an ever closer union among the peoples of Europe, in which decisions are taken as openly as possible and as closely as possible to the citizen."[268] The Treaty has expressed the intention "to enhance further the democratic and efficient functioning of the institutions so as to enable them better to carry out, within a single institutional framework, the tasks entrusted to them".[269] In this perspective important changes have been introduced for Parliament and the Commission.

One should note, concerning Parliament, the extension of co-decision in the legislative acts, and among them the Financial Regulation and the sectoral spending regulations;[270] the new procedures for adopting the annual budget and the multi-annual framework; the right of initiative concerning revision of the Treaties.

But the Treaty also states that the Commission, responsible as a body to the European Parliament,[271] shall now submit "an evaluation report on the Union's finances based on the results achieved".[272] The expectation is that this would be an assessment by the Commission, going further than the traditional record of budgetary implementation.

All this provides ground for the Parliament to seek (and obtain) increased influence in outlining the revised arrangements for EU finances. The setting-up of a special committee to prepare the EU's next long-term budget framework shows the willingness to seize this opportunity.[273]

In particular, one may expect Parliament to recall previous requests such as:

- "A reform of the structure of EU revenue and a reform of the structure of EU expenditure have to go hand-in-hand".[274]
- EU financial resources should be "used for actions with real European added-value, clearly defined priorities and visibility for citizens [and] spent under rules of sound financial management, focusing on efficiency and effectiveness".[275]
- There is a need for "prior identification of positive and negative priorities rather than through self-imposed ceilings"; "it is essential that EU spending be re-evaluated and optimised in order to achieve the highest value-added and most effective EU action"; "it is particularly important that allocations of funds are based on objective criteria and on a continuous evaluation of their performance".[276]
- "An initiative that is insufficiently verifiable should not be financed by public money".[277] And, not least,
- "The Commission has primacy in the management of the Community funds concerned".[278]

The Lisbon Treaty has also upgraded the role of the Commission, from ensuring "the proper functioning and development of the common market" to the more ambitious promotion of "the general interest of the Union".[279] This establishes a link (and a responsibility) with the achievement of the EU objectives as a whole and the need of ensuring consistency, effectiveness and continuity of EU policies and actions.[280]

Concerning the EU budget, the Treaty confirms that it is implemented on the Commission's "own responsibility" and "having regard to the principles of sound financial management".[281] To this effect, the Commission should count on adequate cooperation from member states, with the latter having control and audit obligations in the implementation of the budget and resulting responsibilities. This provision represents a confirmation that member states' bodies must have a key role in the EU budget implementation. It still remains however that it is the Commission that "shall execute the budget *and* manage programmes".[282] This suggests an enhancement of the Commission's role compared to today's situation, in line with the reinforcement of its function as the 'executive' of the Union.

The EU added-value

The European added-value may be said to constitute the keystone of the EU budget edifice. The *raison d'être* of the EU budget cannot be a matter of enthusiasm or faith. Or, be finalised to redistribute money across member states for which one could imagine far-simpler mechanisms. The EU budget's 'legitimacy' in the eyes of the citizens can only be based on clear objectives and convincing achievements.

Indeed, "[a]s a leading principle, the EU budget should be targeted to policies where it can make a difference and bring real added-value."[283] Choices must be explained, understood and accounted for. The more so in a time of great strain on public finances, imposing strict limitations on public spending at all levels. The budget review screening has shown once again a broad acknowledgment that EU spending must be based on an assessment of its added-value.[284] The main question is whether and how a spending programme brings European added-value. Is there 'European added-value' everywhere? What criteria should be used to ensure that the principle of European value added is applied effectively?

The Treaty provides in this respect a number of 'curbs'. It establishes first a causality link between, on the one side, the Union's competences and the objectives to be attained and, on the other side, the financial means necessary to attain these objectives.[285] Second, it indicates that in areas that do not fall within its exclusive competence, the Union's action is restricted to objectives that member states cannot sufficiently achieve themselves but can rather, by reason of the scale or effects, be better achieved at Union level.[286] Third, it explains in support of the previous condition, that "[t]he reasons for concluding that a Union objective can be better achieved at Union level shall be substantiated by qualitative and, wherever possible, quantitative indicators".[287]

As indicated by the Commission, the EU budget should be "targeted to best effect, managed to the highest standards, and that it succeeds in bringing tangible improvements to the daily lives of citizens".[288] This suggests three main characteristics of EU spending added-value:

- *'Catalytic'*. The EU budget is expected to make something happen that would otherwise not happen (or would happen more slowly), i.e. to attain what cannot be matched by national or local spending in acting alone; so that "pooling national resources at EU level can bring major savings for national budgets".[289] However, the European added-value cannot be equated simply to more money available compared to what could normally be provided by national budgets. The 'discriminating' factor for EU spending being not the added-value of spending as such, but rather its 'European' dimension, acting as a catalyst for public and private investors. It is about EU objectives, not 'Europeanised' national objectives.
- *Targeted*. The budget should concentrate on what offers the best added-value and most effective results. It should avoid duplication with national spending but also intervening in all areas of policy-making as if EU spending was a 'magic wand' for all problems. Policies should be assessed against all kinds of costs they entail (for example, those costs imposed upon member states and upon beneficiaries) compared to the objectives. Different EU funding sources should be coordinated. In this context, financial assistance other than grants (for example, EIB loans and other financing facilities) should be considered to leverage the effect of Union funds. But the relative effectiveness of different (non-budgetary) means of intervention available to EU policy-makers, in particular legislative instruments should also be assessed. One should not exclude the possibility that a number of EU policy objectives could be better addressed by improving the regulatory framework than by transferring money across member states.[290]
- *Realistic*. The EU budget should be organised in such a way that the spending meets its goals, through streamlined delivery schemes and a proper account-giving with a single 'owner'.

Whether shared objectives could be better achieved at the European level or at another level is naturally a matter of political choice, involving above all member states and the European Parliament. A thought from J. Monnet seems inspiring in this context: "What must be sought is a fusion of the interest of the European peoples and not merely another effort to maintain an equilibrium of those interests through additional machinery for negotiation".[291]

In any event, the fixed route towards a greater EU added-value passes above all through selectivity, concentration of resources and adequate implementation arrangements. Indeed, "[w]hen ambitious objectives are pursued with limited resources and weak implementation mechanisms, we have a recipe for disappointment".[292]

More money for fewer but achievable objectives

Funds are not unlimited. EU and national spending compete for the same tax revenues. Realism requires an awareness that it is most unlikely that the post-2013 EU funds available will be significantly above the current level.[293] And even cuts should not be excluded as member states attempt to rein in their spending.

However, "it is not only important to discuss the quantity, but also the quality of spending and investment".[294] There are basically two alternatives: more money for a 'few' spending programmes, or less money for a plurality of programmes. In this respect, an indiscriminate horizontal 'cutting' to preserve all existing programmes does not appear to be a sensible solution.[295] The advantage of this 'conservative' approach would be confined to an accounting matching with the available resources, further compounding the current lack of critical mass. One should also consider the EU budget in a broader perspective, by looking at European and national budgets together. Less funds from the EU budget do not mean necessarily less funds for a given policy, but rather the choice for a different level of government.[296]

The priority seems to be to 'prioritisation', involving most likely hard political choices.[297] In this context the argument that the EU budget is relatively 'small' has its best value. This 'constraint' is actually a potential means of giving more significance and credibility to EU action by putting in place an evidence-based decision-making process to support such choices.

The starting-point of all administration is "the balance-sheet of needs and resources".[298] To ensure that "our proposals really do deliver what they promise and to enable us to revise and correct them where they fail to work as expected",[299] the obvious way out is an assessment of (past and future) policies, taking stock of the significant experience and evaluation work available in the present spending areas. This should allow us to design spending programmes in terms of specific, measurable and achievable objectives, expected outcomes and resulting costs.[300] In this respect a 'critical mass' of necessary funds constitutes a crucial factor to achieve a precise and identifiable result.[301] In its turn, accountability can only be enhanced by establishing a link between investment costs and expected benefits.

This means that the volume of funds allocated to the EU budget should result from an assessment of the costs of specific objectives achievable with the available funds. While still being compatible with an overall ceiling on EU revenue, the EU budget would thus enhance its function as an instrument of action and potential achievements, as opposed to pre-agreed 'budgetary balance'-driven intergovernmental redistribution.

Putting the emphasis on achievable objectives rather than on processes would also put the basis for a shift from 'eligible' inputs of spending towards outputs and outcomes. This would make unnecessary 'absorption-addicting' rules like the N+2 (or N+3) rule in the Cohesion policy. And it would pave the way to a combination of sunset clauses providing for the discontinuation of spending programmes without meaningful results after a certain period of time, and incentives to reward best performers.[302] This approach addresses one of the present 'taboos': the lack of conditionality for results. One should welcome in this respect that one of the key conclusions of the Commission concerning the EU budget review is the need for a results-driven budget (as opposed to inputs-based), where spending programmes must have a real impact.[303] A first signal in this respect is represented by the initiative recently taken by the Commission in the research field, moving away from a cost-based system focused on inputs towards a system of funding based on prior definition and acceptance of outputs/outcomes.[304] Also, a shift from inputs of eligible spending to results will make it possible to define control systems in a broader perspective, taking account of 'value for money' concerns and thus enhancing their added-value for the management.

In line with the 'targeted' nature of the EU added-value and the 'special' role of the EU budget as a functional instrument for realising actions that could not otherwise be effectively implemented by the national level, consideration should be given to using EU funds to 'realise' well-defined actions that undeniably belong to the EU level. In other words, to provide 'the cake rather than the icing'. The 'complementarity' or 'additionality' of the EU budget would come to light not so much by adding 'something' to a number of existing policies already financed by national budgets, but, above all, by realising *in toto* projects that are 'European' by definition and could therefore, in some way, be considered as an exclusive priority of that level.

EU budget, what 'phone number'?

The natural outcome of a virtuous process where objectives are clear, agreed and achievable is an unequivocal ownership as a precondition for both achieving policy objectives and ensuring 'value for money'. This would also lead to an accountability process "based on obligations to demonstrate, review, and take responsibility for performance, both the results achieved in light of agreed expectations and the means used".[305]

As pointed out in the Commission's Budget review consultation paper, "a fresh look needs to be taken to determine how different types of management can offer sound financial management and whether the existing balance represents the right answer".[306] Nowadays, the interpretation given to the subsidiarity/proportionality principles implies that 'shared management' arrangements are based on a dissociation of the decision-taking aspect from the financial implementation. Such a framework creates the conditions for diffused responsibilities and, in practice, for 'immunity' of the management actors as the main management and control functions are implemented by national bodies not directly accountable at EU level. The Commission, which in theory bears ultimate responsibility, is not in the position to commit itself to anything under member states' responsibilities as it lacks the necessary authority. In this respect, any clearance mechanisms it may apply constitute at most an *ex-post* funds recovery and not a 'policy-oriented' function.

For both constitutional and political reasons, there is a natural sensitivity to any form of accountability of national bodies towards EU institutions. In particular, it does not seem realistic to put in place a formal accountability process before the European Parliament, for example in the framework of the discharge procedure. In the end, this would mean making national governments accountable to both national parliaments and the European Parliament, a possibility that member states have always dismissed, insisting on keeping the Commission's ultimate responsibility set in the Treaty. The alternative to run such a process at national level and in a national context (each member state responsible for the EU funds spent within its territory) seems actually to prefigure a different scenario, equating the EU added-value to 'more money' rather than a project of achieving EU objectives with EU funds. It would lead in practice to a 'nationalisation' of the EU budget, thus calling into question its very necessity.

As the Commission observed, it must "be clearer who is responsible for policy execution. This constitutes the pre-condition for making the EU system more open and accountable to all European citizens." Since it is about placing public resources in common to achieve common EU objectives, it is legitimate to expect that the management of EU funds takes place through an effective EU-driven process, ending-up in a full accountability at EU level. To counter the present diffusion of responsibilities and as a result of an enhanced concept of EU added-value, there seems to be no alternative but to designate the Commission as the single master for the EU budget implementation as a whole. This full incumbency, following a political mandate, should lay in its hands whatever the management mode. Its competence to "execute the budget and manage programmes" should be instrumental in fulfilling its main role of promoting the general interest of the Union.[307]

In a future perspective, where one might look more to results than to inputs of spending, the Commission will have to demonstrate that it has done everything possible to achieve the intended results, 'making the difference' when compared to purely national spending. And that it has learned from past experience what works and does not work. Indeed, the primary purpose of accountability is not to cast blame and to punish. It should rather help in identifying lessons for the future, to make future approaches more relevant and effective.

For this to happen, a precondition is the alignment of the Commission's tasks, powers and responsibilities. There is no need to transform the Commission into a kind of 'Colossus of Brussels', with hundreds of thousands of officials replacing functions presently carried out by national bodies. This would not be feasible in practice, certainly not cost-effective and in any event not politically realistic. National bodies should remain an essential element of the EU delivery system. There is however room for reflection on "where the balance should lie between EU-level tools and national level tools, and what expectations should be placed on Member States implementing EU policy in their own countries."[308]

Experience shows that remote administration, devoid of implementation constraints and responsibilities, increases formalism and complexity at the expense of substance. Systems 'modelling', pursued through increasingly tight provisions and sustained by a number of prescriptions and interdictions, cannot make up for insufficient supervision. It is indeed quicker and easier to develop and pass legal provisions than to build effective implementing institutions (Sigma, 1998:6).

To avoid an implementation gap, i.e. a deficit between the set of legal norms and the capacity to implement and enforce them according to EU standards, it seems logical that as a consequence of the Commission's full incumbency in the EU budget implementation, national bodies dealing with EU funds should act on behalf of the Commission. The delegation to national bodies should then be understood as covering specific executive tasks only, not the budgetary implementation as such.[309] This would require some form of accreditation and 'contract' based upon pre-specified output and performance targets and budgetary allocations, in line with the EU objectives selected.[310] It is only if there is 'one' implementation line (and not as many as there are national bodies) that one can sustain the Commission's ultimate responsibility, which cannot itself be subject to delegation.

The idea of an accreditation by the EU of national systems is not new. Its main components were embedded in EU rules until recent years. Assurance on systems should become a pre-condition for allocation and management of EU funds; i.e. administrative structures at national level should be assessed (at operational level) as adequate to deliver the outcomes expected. The aim is to ascertain their capacities to 'absorb' funds effectively, by putting forward, managing and maintaining meaningful projects in line with the pre-agreed policy objectives. This means the establishment by the Commission of 'stress tests' as overseer of national bodies operating in the framework of the EU budget.

Such an 'accreditation process' would not be incompatible with an eventual 'geographical' allocation of funds to member states, providing that these funds will be used only by the 'certified' bodies. A 'selective' process of identification of national bodies for EU spending (a kind of 'Champions league') would introduce an element of 'reward' and sound external pressure, which in the end should benefit public spending also at the national level.[311] As compared to the present financial corrective mechanisms, whose effectiveness as deterrent is questionable, a 'disqualification' with consequent loss of the 'certification' for managing

EU funds would be a reputational sanction far more effective and dissuasive.

The current implementation logic should be reversed, with a shift from the present '*ex-post*' (first pay out the money, then time will tell) to '*ex-ante*' (prevention is better than the cure). In short, from a substantially passive oversight to a more active one.[312] There should no longer be a segregation of functions between the EU and the national level, but a true 'sharing' of roles under one single responsibility. This means putting an end to the dissociation of the decision-taking aspect from the financial implementation.

Partnership with national bodies should not be limited to an exchange of plans, reports and reimbursement claims. It should involve co-decision in the EU meaning, with a weighting proportional to the funds committed for achieving a given objective. This would imply for example that the setting-up and the management of the programmes implemented in shared management arrangements will no longer be left solely in the hands of the member states. And that at the very least the Commission is made aware and is prepared to endorse directly that what is intended to be achieved responds to the criteria of EU added-value.[313]

The EU authorising officer would therefore be truly responsible "for implementing revenue and expenditure in accordance with the principles of sound financial management and for ensuring that the requirements of legality and regularity are complied with"; and it should be accountable for "the results of the operations by reference to the objectives set" as well as "the use made of the resources provided".[314] In this connection, only a full awareness of the Commission on the EU budget implementation may ensure practical relevance to the new provision of establishing each year an evaluation report on the Union's finances based on the results achieved by EU funds.[315]

Like the port pilot, the EU Commission would not be the owner of the boat but would retain responsibility to take it safely to port. A clearer management line under the Commission's responsibility would put an end to the shuttling back and forth of responsibilities between national and EU level. And, not least, as indeed accountability is closely linked to parliamentary control, it will give full dignity to the EU discharge procedure. Contrary to the today's situation, the Commission would be in the position to respond on the actual use of the funds and the results achieved.

Concluding remarks

The above considerations attempt to provide a tentative response to the difficulties of the present EU budget system at the origin of the present accountability gap. The prejudice is that a 'quantum leap' is needed. The resulting framework should be considered in a prospective dimension and in a fundamentally different context than the present one.

The sketched framework would admittedly go far further than the one in place today. It would end up in practice first for the Commission to establish a kind of 'rating' of systems prior to bidding for EU money. An inevitable result could be that not all bodies that are dealing today with EU funds would finally prove fit for the task. And then, as the owner of the EU budget implementation, it would involve the Commission taking part in the decision process, although in partnership with national bodies. This would require adopting a functional understanding of the principles of subsidiarity and proportionality to make room for a different governance system. Also, a 'gear change' for the Commission would be necessary, with a different balance of skills in its services and an adapted project management approach.

The recently presented Commission's conclusions on the EU budget reform constitute a comprehensive illustration of the present difficulties. Sensitive proposals are put forward as a basis for a better post-2013 EU budget. The debate on the EU future finances has however only started and its outcome is clearly unpredictable today. It will however undoubtedly serve as a 'litmus test' of the European project as a whole.

References

Auditor General of Canada (2002), *Modernizing accountability in the public sector*, Ch. 9, December.

Bachtler. J. and C. Mendez (2010), *Administrative Reform and Unintended Consequences: An Assessment of the EU Cohesion Policy 'Audit Explosion'*, *Journal of European Public Policy*, forthcoming.

Barlev, B. (2006), "A Biblical statement of accountability", *Accounting History*, Vol. 11, No. 2, pp. 173-197.

Barroso, J.M. (2008), address to the conference on Reforming the Budget, Changing Europe, 12 November (http://ec.europa.eu/budget/reform/library/conference/intro_president.pdf).

---------- (2009), Political guidelines for the next Commission, 3 September (http://ec.europa.eu/commission_2010-2014/president/pdf/press_20090903_en.pdf).

--------- (2010), State of the Union 2010, speech, 7 September, (SPEECH/10/411, http://europa.eu/rapid/pressReleasesAction.do?reference=SPEECH/10/411&format=HTML&aged=0&language=EN&guiLanguage=en).

Begg, I., N. Grimwade and P. Price (1997), *Les ressources propres de l'Union européenne: analyse et développements possibles,* Working Document, European Parliament, September.

Begg, I., H. Enderlein, J. Le Cacheux and M. Mrak (2008), *Financing of the European Union Budget,* Study for European Commission, Final Report, April.

Bemelmans-Videc, M.L. and J. Lonsdale (2007), *Accountability - the challenges for two professions,* in M.L. Bemelmans-Videc, J. Lonsdale and B. Perrin (eds), Making accountability work: Dilemmas for evaluation and for audit, Transaction Publishers.

Bird, R. and M. Smart (2001), "Intergovernmental Fiscal Transfers: Some Lessons from International Experience", mimeo, March.

Bovens, M. (2007), *Public accountability,* in E. Ferlie, L. Lynn and C. Pollitt (eds), *The Oxford Handbook of Public Management,* Oxford: Oxford University Press.

---------- (2006), *Analysing and assessing public accountability. A conceptual framework*, European Governance Papers No. C-06-01, January.

Brandsma, G.J. (2007), *Accountability deficits in European 'Comitology' decision-making*, European Integration online Papers (EIoP) Vol. 11 (2007) No. 4, 25 May (http://eiop.or.at/eiop/texte/2007-004a.htm).

Broeksteeg H., I. Van den Driessch and L. Verhey, L. (eds) (2008), *Political accountability in Europe, which way forward*, Europa Law Publishing, March.

Cassese, S. (2006), *Four Features of the European Administrative Space*, paper presented to the Connex thematic conference Towards a European Administrative Space, Birbeck College, University of London, 16-18 November (http://www.mzes.uni-mannheim.de/projekte/typo3/site/fileadmin/research%20groups/crosscutting/Papers_London_Nov2006/Cassese.pdf).

Carmona, S., and M. Ezzamel (2005), *Accounting and forms of accountability in ancient civilizations: Mesopotamia and ancient Egypt*, IE Working Paper WP05-21, IE Business School, Madrid, May.

Cattoir, P. (2004), *Tax-based EU own resources: An assessment*, Working Paper No. 1/2004, DG for Taxation and Customs Union, European Commission, April.

CEPS, EGMONT and EPC (2007), *The Treaty of Lisbon: Implementing the institutional innovations*, Brussels, November.

Cipriani, G. (2007), *Rethinking the EU Budget: Three Unavoidable Reforms*, CEPS Paperback, Brussels, November.

Committee of Independent Experts (1999), *First Report on Allegations Regarding Fraud, Mismanagement and Nepotism in the European Commission*, Brussels, 15 March.

---------- (1999), *Second Report on Reform of the Commission: Analysis of current practice and proposals for tackling mismanagement, irregularities and fraud*, Brussels, 10 September.

Committee on Standards in Public Life, *The Seven Principles of Public Life* (http://www.public-standards.org.uk/About/The_7_Principles.html).

Dyrberg P. (2002), *Accountability and Legitimacy: What is the Contribution of Transparency?*, in A. Arnull and D. Wincott (eds), *Accountability and Legitimacy in the European Union*, Oxford: Oxford University Press.

European Commission (1965) *Financement de la politique agricole commune - Ressources propres de la Communauté – Renforcement des pouvoirs du Parlement européen*, COM(65) 150, 31 March.

---------- (1977), *Report by the Study Group on the Role of Public Finance in European Integration*, Rapporteurs: D. MacDougal et al., Luxembourg, April.

---------- (1978), *Global appraisal of the budgetary problems of the Community*, COM(78) 64, 27 February.

---------- (1998), *Financing the European Union*, Commission Report on the Operation of the Own Resources System, 7 October.

---------- (2001), *European Governance, a White Paper*, COM (428) 2001, 25 July.

---------- (2002), *A project for the European Union*, Communication from the Commission, COM(2002) 247, 22 May (http://eurlex.europa.eu/LexUriServ/LexUriServ.do?uri=COM:2002:0247:FIN:EN:PDF).

---------- (2003), Directorate-General Regional Policy, *A Study of the Efficiency of the Implementation Methods for Structural Funds*, December (http://ec.europa.eu/regional_policy/sources/docgener/studies/pdf/3cr/efficiency_methods_full.pdf).

---------- (2004), *Financial Perspectives 2007-13*, Communication to the Council and the European Parliament, COM(2004) 487 final, 14 July.

---------- (2006), *Communication on Enlargement Strategy and Main Challenges 2006–07*, COM(2006) 649, 8 November.

---------- (2008), *EU Public Finance* (http://ec.europa.eu/budget/library/publications/financial_pub/EU_pub_fin_en.pdf).

---------- (2009), *Report by the Study Group on an Agenda for a reformed Cohesion policy*, Rapporteur: F. Barca, Brussels, April (http://ec.europa.eu/regional_policy/policy/future/barca_en.htm)

---------- (2010), Eurobarometer 70, Public opinion in the European Union (October-November 2008), June.

European Parliament (1973) - *The case for a European Audit Office, Introduction by Heinrich Aigner, Vice-Chairman of the Committee on Budgets* - Luxembourg, Office for Official Publications of the European Communities, September.

---------- (2010), "From the Schuman Declaration to the birth of the ECSC: The role of Jean Monnet", *Cardoc Journals*, No. 6, May.

Gretschmann, K. (1998), *Reform of the Own-Resources system and net positions in the EU budget*, Working Document, European Parliament, October.

Gros, D. (2008), *How to Achieve a Better Budget for the European Union*, paper presented at the Conference on Public Finances in the EU, European Commission, Brussels, 3-4 April (http://ec.europa.eu/dgs/policy_advisers/conference_docs/gros_bepa_conference_final.pdf).

Harlow, C. (2002a), *Accountability and European Governance*, in *Accountability in the European Union*, Oxford: Oxford University Press.

---------- (2002b), *Thinking about Accountability*, in *Accountability in the European Union*, Oxford: Oxford University Press.

Hübner, D. (2007a), *European Regional Policy: History, Achievements and Perspectives*, speech 07/542, Lunch Debate on the 50th Anniversary of the EU, 17 September, Brussels.

---------- (2007b), speech at seminar on The Future of Public Audit in the EU, European Court of Auditors, Luxembourg, 18 October, document ECA/07/22.

Laffan, B. (2003), *Auditing and accountability in the European Union, Journal of European Public Policy*, October.

Lenaerts, K., (1991), *Some reflections on the separation of powers in the European Community, Common Market Law Review*, Vol. 28, No. 1.

Mattessich, R. (1998), *Recent Insights into Mesopotamian Accounting of the 3rd Millennium B.C. – Successor to Token Accounting, Accounting Historians Journal*, Vol. 25, No. 1, June.

McCubbins, M. and Schwartz T. (1984), *Congressional oversight overlooked: police patrols versus fire alarms, American Journal of Political Science*, Vol. 28, No 1, February.

Monnet, J. (1978), *Memoirs*, London: Collins.

Power, M. (1997), *The Audit Society: Rituals of Verification*, Oxford: Oxford University Press.

Pisani, E. (1956), *Administration de gestion, administration de mission, Revue française de science politique*, Vol. 6, No. 2.

Ponzano, P. (2009), *Brèves considerations sur le rôle de la Commission européenne, Revue du Droit de l'Union Européenne*, No. 2.

Schenker-Wicki, A. (2006), "Do controls improve performance", in *Tolerable risk of error in underlying transactions, tolerable for whom?*, Workshop proceedings of the Committee on Budgetary Control of the EU

Parliament, Brussels, July (http://www.europarl.europa.eu/comparl/cont/site/auditions/workshop/schenker.pdf).

Schön-Quinlivan, E. (2006), *Preparing for EU enlargement: an analysis of the institutional change and administrative reform in the EU Commission (1958-2000),* EU-consent (http://www.eu-consent.net/library/Award_Winner3.pdf).

Seabright, P. (1996), *Accountability and Decentralization in Government: an Incomplete Contracts Model, European Economic Review,* 40.

Šemeta, A. (2010), speech on Discharge and Audit at the meeting of the Parliamentary Committee on Budgetary Control, 22 February (http://ec.europa.eu/commission_2010-2014/semeta/headlines/speeches/2010/02/cocobu_220210%20.pdf).

Shah, A. (2004), *Fiscal Decentralization in Developing and Transition Economies,* World Bank Policy Research Working Paper No. 3282, World Bank, Washington, D.C., April.

Sigma (1998), *Preparing public administrations for the European Administrative Space,* Sigma Paper No. 23, OECD, Paris, May.

---------- (1999), *European Principles For Public Administration,* Sigma Paper No. 27, OECD, Paris, November.

---------- (2007), *Organising the central State administration,* Sigma Paper No. 43, OECD, Paris, June.

Starling, G. (2008), *Managing the Public Sector,* Thomson Wadsworth.

Tarschys, D. (2005), *The Enigma of European Added Value,* Swedish Institute for European Policy Studies, Stockholm, June.

van Gerven, W. (2007), *Political, ethical and financial and legal responsibility of EU Commissioners,* contribution presented at the public hearing on Governance in the European Commission, European Parliament Committee on Budgetary Control, 3-4 October.

Annex: National Control & Reporting Functions

Control system for agriculture (direct expenditure)

Member state's body	Control functions	Reporting and certification obligations
Paying agency	Provides sufficient guarantees that: • the admissibility of claims and compliance with EU rules are checked before payment is authorised; and • the payments effected are correctly and fully recorded in the accounts. The systems generally provide for exhaustive *ex-ante* administrative controls of 100% of the aid applications, cross-checks with other databases where this is considered appropriate as well as pre-payment on-the-spot controls of a sample of transactions ranging between 1% and 100% (normally between 5% and 10%), depending on the risk associated with the regime in question. If the on-the-spot controls reveal a high number of irregularities, additional controls must be carried out. *Ex-post* controls are carried out in accordance with an annual audit plan established on the basis of a pre-determined audit strategy.	The head of the paying agency provides the annual accounts of the accredited paying agency accompanied by a Statement of Assurance with a declaration on the completeness, accuracy and veracity of the accounts and that a system is in place that provides reasonable assurance on the legality and regularity of the underlying transactions.

Certifying body	Independent body responsible for certifying reasonable assurance that the accounts transmitted to the Commission are true, complete and accurate and that the internal control procedures have operated satisfactorily. Examines the paying agency's administrative structures and procedures as well as a sample of transactions. This examination covers the question whether the paying agency's administrative structure is capable of ensuring that compliance with EU rules is checked before any payments are made. In broad terms, Certifying bodies are not required to verify activities at the level of the final beneficiary. The responsibilities do not extend to checking that claims for payment of subsidy are correct.	Establishes an opinion on the paying agency's Statement of Assurance and Declaration, stating whether: • the paying agency complies with the accreditation criteria; • the paying agency's procedures are such as to give reasonable assurance that the expenditure was effected in compliance with EU rules; • the annual accounts are in accordance with the paying agency's books and records; • the statement of expenditure and intervention operations are materially true, complete and accurate; • the financial interests of the EU are properly protected; and • Verifies and validates IACS statistics.
Coordinating body	If the member state has more than one paying agency, it acts as the Commission's sole interlocutor for all questions regarding the management and control of agricultural expenditure.	Produces an annual summary (synthesis report) of all Statements of Assurance and of all certificates from the certification bodies.

National control system for Cohesion policy

Member state's body	Control functions	Reporting and certification obligations
Managing authority	• Makes sure that operations selected for the programme comply with the criteria and rules applicable. • Verifies that products and services are delivered and that the expenditure declared by the beneficiaries for operations has actually been incurred and complies with EU and national rules. This implies both desk checks (on documents such as lists of invoices and progress or final reports accompanying payment claims from project promoters) and on-the-spot visits to projects selected using a sound sampling methodology. • Corrects irregular expenditure found by withdrawing it from payment claims to the Commission and recovering grants already paid from the beneficiaries.	Delivers an annual performance report to the Commission showing the progress made in implementing the operational programme and its financial implementation. A final report must also be delivered no later than 31 March 2017.
Certifying authority	• Examines the expenditure claims transmitted by the Managing Authority. It assesses reliance of the information on the latter's verifications of the beneficiaries. It also takes account of the available Audit Authority reports on the functioning of the control systems. • It may carry out additional checks itself or ask others to do so.	Certifies to the Commission that the expenditure being declared for reimbursement is accurate, results from a reliable accounting system, and is compliant with applicable EU and national rules.

Audit authority	• On the basis of an audit strategy approved by the Commission, verifies the effectiveness of the work done by the Managing and Certifying Authorities in order to determine whether risks remain that irregular expenditure could be certified. • Its work is based on a standard methodology built on systems assessments and supported by substantive testing of project expenditure declared over a 12-month reference period.	Provides an annual control report to the Commission setting out the findings of the audits carried out during the previous year. This is accompanied by an audit opinion as to whether reasonable assurance exists that statements of expenditure presented to the Commission are correct. Submits to the Commission at the latest by 31 March 2017 a closure declaration assessing the validity of the application for payment of the final balance and the legality and regularity of the underlying transactions covered by the final statement of expenditure, which shall be supported by a final control report.

Notes

[1] See the Code of Hammurabi (§ 233), translation by L.W. King (available at http://avalon.law.yale.edu/ancient/hamframe.asp). The Code of Hammurabi is a collection of the King of Babylon's laws [1795-1750 BC].

[2] Barlev (2006:176) refers in this respect to the accounting method of comparing theoretical (expected) and actual performance used in Mesopotamia and referred to as "budgetary procedure" by Mattessich (1998).

[3] See Book of Exodus (Ex. 38:21–31), cited in Barlev (2006:192).

[4] See the Holy Gospel according to St. Luke (16.1-2/13).

[5] See Art. 15 of the Declaration of the Rights of Man and the Citizen (National Assembly of France, 26 August 1789). A similar definition has been adopted by the Committee on Standards in Public Life, an independent advisory body to the UK Government. The definition reads: "Holders of public office are accountable for their decisions and actions to the public and must submit themselves to whatever scrutiny is appropriate to their office".

[6] Together with openness, participation, effectiveness and coherence, the European Commission (2001:10) has defined accountability as one of the five principles underpinning good governance. Although there are no EU rules (thus an *acquis communautaire*) regarding administrative organisation or public management, shared principles of public administration among EU member states progressively resulted from the jurisprudence of the European Court of Justice, so as to put in place the conditions for an 'European Administrative Space' (EAS). The EAS represents an evolving process of increasing convergence between national administrative legal orders and administrative practices of member states, enforced in practice through administrative laws and procedures. One should also notice that the Charter of Fundamental Rights of the European Union (OJ C 303 of 14.12.2007) recognises (in its Art. 41) the right to "good administration" as one of the EU fundamental citizens' rights. The Treaty on European Union (TEU), Art. 6 (1), has given to the Charter of Fundamental Rights the same legal value as the Treaties.

[7] The principal-agent partnership model constitutes in essence a hierarchical relationship in which objectives and policies are set by the principal and implementation by the agent is closely supervised and monitored. Standard management-by-objectives models and methods provide the means of making this type of partnership work (see Sigma, 1998:51).

[8] See Committee of Independent Experts (1999, Vol. II, point 7.14.5, p. 130).

[9] This concept is close to the definition of 'political responsibility' given by van Gerven (2007:2).

[10] For example, in the EU Financial Regulation, the words "responsibility" and "accountability" are used interchangeably, although with a marked preference for the first (see Council Regulation (EC, Euratom) No. 1605/2002 of 25 June 2002 on the Financial Regulation applicable to the general budget of the European Communities, OJ L 248, 16.9.2002, as amended last by Council Regulation (EC) No. 1525/2007 of 17 December 2007, OJ L 343, 17.12.2007).

[11] "*E Pluribus Unum*", the concept of 'many' becoming 'one', is embedded in the seal of the United States of America. It refers to the union between the states and federal government in a single nation.

[12] The principle of 'economy' requires that the resources used shall be made available in due time, in appropriate quantity and quality and at the best price. 'Efficiency' is characteristically a managerial value consisting in essence of maintaining a good ratio between resources employed and results attained. A related value is 'effectiveness', which basically consists of ensuring that the performance of public administration is successful in achieving the goals and solving the public problems set for it by law and government (see Sigma, 1999:13). These principles (known as the 'three E's') are also codified in the EU Financial Regulation under the concept of sound financial management (see Art. 27 of the Financial Regulation, Council Regulation (EC, Euratom) No. 1605/2002, op. cit.).

[13] See the GAO website (http://www.gao.gov/about/index.html).

[14] See the European Court of Auditors' "Mission, Vision, Values and Strategic Objectives" (http://eca.europa.eu/portal/pls/portal/docs/1/5544724.PDF).

[15] See Auditor General of Canada (2002:5).

[16] See Art. 1 TEU. It should also be noted that the Treaty of Lisbon has abandoned the constitutional concept which consisted of repealing all existing Treaties and replacing them by a single text called "Constitution" as provided by the (not ratified) Constitutional Treaty signed on 29.10.2004 (OJ C310 of 16.12.2004).

[17] See Art. 3(6) TEU.

[18] See Art. 5(1) and (2) TEU. Art. 2 of the Treaty on the Functioning of the European Union (TFEU) establishes three categories of EU competences depending on the intervention field (exclusive, shared with the member states, and competence to carry out actions to support, coordinate or supplement members states' actions). In few areas the European Union has exclusive competence (see Art. 3 TFEU). Most of EU competences are shared with member states (see Art. 4 TFEU). It is worth mentioning that Art. 4(1) TEU (and the Declaration No. 18 in relation to the delimitation of competences attached to the Treaty of Lisbon) underlines that "competences not conferred upon the Union in the Treaties remain with the Member States". Protocol No. 25 on the exercise of shared competence clarifies that "when the Union has taken action in a certain area, the scope of this exercise of

competence only covers those elements governed by the Union act in question and therefore does not cover the whole area". An increase or a reduction of EU competences may be decided in accordance with the Treaty's ordinary revision procedure provided for in Art. 48 TEU. The procedure may be initiated by member states, the European Parliament or the Commission. A Treaty revision would require ratification by member states in accordance with their respective constitutional requirements.

[19] The principles of subsidiarity and proportionality were set out by the Treaty of Maastricht (1992) as general principles of EU law. The principle of subsidiarity had some historical antecedents in the European Coal and Steel Community (ECSC) Treaty of 1951 (Art. 5) and in the Single European Act of 1986 (Art. 130r(4)). The overall approach has been developed by the conclusions of the Presidency at the European Council of Edinburgh (11-12 December 1992). Subsequently, the European Parliament, the Council and the Commission concluded in November 1993 an Inter-institutional Agreement on procedures for implementing the principle of subsidiarity (OJ C 329, 6.12.1993, p. 132). Furthermore, the Treaty of Amsterdam (1997) introduced the protocols on the application of the principles of subsidiarity and proportionality as well as on the role of national Parliaments in the European Union. This encouraged greater involvement of national Parliaments in EU activities and enhanced their ability to express their views on matters that may be of particular interest to them. The importance of the subsidiarity and proportionality principles has been further stressed by the Treaty of Lisbon. A Protocol (No. 2) on the application of the principles of subsidiarity and proportionality provides that national Parliaments may express their opinions with regard to the compliance of a legislative act with the principle of subsidiarity and ask for it to be reviewed. The same protocol also provides for national Parliaments and the Committee of the Regions to bring suspected violations of the principle of subsidiarity before the European Court of Justice. One may also note that a 'subsidiarity monitoring network' has been created by the Committee of the Regions in order to facilitate the exchange of information between local and regional authorities in the European Union and the EU level. This regards the various policy documents and proposals of the European Commission which, once adopted, will have a direct impact on local and regional authorities and the policies for which they are responsible (see http://subsidiarity.cor.europa.eu/Help/tabid/283/Default.aspx). Each year the Commission presents a report on the application of the principles of subsidiarity and proportionality (for the latest report, see COM (2010) 547 final of 8.10.2010).

[20] See Art. 5(3) TEU.

[21] See Art. 5(4) TEU.

[22] See European Commission (2002:24).

[23] Lenaerts indicates that the common understanding of the principle of separation of powers, i.e. a distinction between those who hold the legislative, executive and judicial power, is not practicable in the EU because of a lack of a clear-cut line between the legislative and the executive branches of the EU government. But this is not to say that the separation of powers is meaningless in the EU context, but rather that its understanding should be a functional one. The author stresses that while the legislative function is normally performed by EU Institutions, the executive and judicial functions are performed to a large extent by member states on behalf of the EU. Cassese (2006) has pointed out four specific features of the EU framework compared with domestic administrative orders. Firstly, contrary to domestic administrations, the European administration has not just one centre of power but two. These are an intergovernmental body (the Council) and a purely European institution (the Commission). Second, while domestic administrations have exclusive powers of implementation, the consequence of the subsidiarity principle is that the European administration is not the only implementing authority of the EU. The implementing power of the EU is consequently residual and not monopolistic. So, domestic administrations must facilitate and implement European law (a formal recognition of this principle can be found in Art. 4(3) TEU). Thirdly, while domestic administrative law is binomial (i.e. there are relations between two poles, the executive and a private party), European administrative law is trinomial. There are relations among the European Commission, national administrations and private parties, and each may play multiple roles. This multiplicity of players generates "polycentric adjudication processes". Finally, while domestic administrative law is usually a privileged branch of law, full of executive prerogatives, in European administrative law the administration does not generally enjoy special rights and privileges.

[24] See European Commission (2002:20).

[25] See the Preamble of the Treaty on European Union. Art. 13(1) TEU reads: "The Union shall have an institutional framework which shall aim to promote its values, advance its objectives, serve its interests, those of its citizens and those of the Member States, and ensure the consistency, effectiveness and continuity of its policies and actions."

[26] See case-law 26/62, NV Algemene Transport- en Expeditie Onderneming van Gend & Loos v Netherlands Inland Revenue Administration. Judgment of the Court of 5 February 1963, ECR 1963, p. 1 and Case-law 6/64, Flaminio Costa v E.N.E.L.. Judgment of the Court of 15 July 1964, ECR 1964, p. 1251.

[27] See Case-law 103/88, Fratelli Costanzo SpA v Comune di Milano. Judgment of the Court of 22 June 1989. ECR 1989, p. 1839, para. 33.

[28] See Art. 13(2) TEU. One may notice that the Treaty reiterates the limits of powers of each institution "with particular regard to the Union's own resources and the balance between revenue and expenditure" (see Art. 314(10) TFEU). One should also note that the European Court of Justice has dismissed the argument that all original law-making power is vested in the Council, whilst the Commission has only powers of surveillance and implementation. The Court has judged that there is no basis for this argument as according to the Treaties the Commission is to participate in carrying out the tasks entrusted to the Community on the same basis as the other Institutions, each acting within the limits of the powers conferred upon it by the Treaty (see Joined Cases-law 188 to 190/80, French Republic, Italian Republic and United Kingdom of Great Britain and Northern Ireland v Commission of the European Communities. Judgment of the Court of 6 July 1982, ECR 1982, p. 2545).

[29] See Art. 15(1) TEU.

[30] See Arts 14(1), 16(1) and 17(2) TEU. Following entering into force of the Treaty of Lisbon, almost all EU legislation will be endorsed by both the Parliament and Council through the ordinary legislative procedure (see Art. 294 TFEU). The latter's field of application, previously known as "co-decision", has more than doubled, applying to existing EU policies (like agriculture and fisheries, Structural Funds, immigration and judicial cooperation) or new areas like energy, space and tourism.

[31] See Arts 17(1) TEU, 290 and 291 TFEU. Reference is made to the distinction between delegated acts (the Commission to adopt delegated acts in the field of competence of the European Parliament and/or the Council, Art. 290 TFEU) and implementing acts (acts adopted by the Commission in its own field of competence, Art. 291 TFEU). Under the EC Treaty it was the Council that could confer implementing powers on the Commission. The Council could also reserve implementing powers to itself in specific cases. The new Treaty put the co-legislators on an equal footing in relation to the conferral of delegated and implementing powers. See also note 104.

[32] See Art. 10(2) TEU. The Council consist "of a representative of each Member State at ministerial level, who may commit the government of the Member State in question and cast its vote" (see Art. 16(2) TEU).

[33] See Art. 16(1) TEU. It is worth mentioning in this respect the declaration made by the German Chancellor K. Adenauer on 9 September 1952, at the inaugural meeting of the ECSC Council, as reported by J. Monnet: "The Council stands at the crossroads of two kinds of sovereignty, national and supranational...While it must safeguard the national interests of the member States, it must not regard this as its

paramount task. Its paramount task is to promote the interests of the Community; and unless it does so, the Community will not develop" (Monnet, 1978:381).

[34] See Art. 10(1) and (2) TEU.

[35] See Art. 14(1) TEU. In this respect Parliament has the faculty to hear the European Council, the Council and the Commission (see Art. 230 TFEU).

[36] See Art. 17(1) TEU. This principle has been introduced by the Lisbon Treaty but was already embedded in the Commission's Governance Statement of 30.5.2007. This stance has been recalled by European Commission President José Manuel Barroso, stating that "[o]nly the Commission has the authority, the administrative capacity and the technical expertise to make proposals that take the interests of all Member States and all citizens into account, and the long-term view needed to tackle the big issues we face today" (see European Commission President José Manuel Barroso, Political guidelines for the next Commission, 3 September 2009, p. 37). As pointed out by Ponzano (2009:218) the general interest of the Union does not necessarily correspond to the addition of national interests, neither it equates the lowest common denominator of the different national stances.

[37] See Art. 17(1) TEU. As observed earlier (see note 23) the executive and judicial functions are performed to a large extent by member states on behalf of the EU. As a kind of *ultima ratio*, when the Commission considers that a member state has failed to fulfil a Treaty obligation, it may bring the matter before the Court of Justice seeking a declaration of an infringement of EU law. The Commission can apply to the Court a second time seeking the application of financial sanctions until the first ruling of the Court is respected (see Arts 258 and 260 TFEU).

[38] See Art. 17(1) TEU.

[39] See Art. 17(2) TEU. The Treaty on the Functioning of the European Union (see Art. 289(4)) provides that in specific cases legislative acts may be adopted on the initiative of a group of member states or of the European Parliament, on a recommendation from the European Central Bank or at the request of the Court of Justice or the European Investment Bank. For example, in the area of judicial cooperation in criminal matters and of the police cooperation acts may be adopted on the initiative of a quarter of the member states (see Art. 76 TFEU). Both the European Parliament and the Council may request the Commission to submit any appropriate proposal and, if the Commission disagrees, to justify its position (see Arts 225 and 241 TFEU). The Treaty also provides that a group of not less than one million EU citizens may ask the Commission to draw up a proposal (see Art. 11(4) TEU).

[40] See Arts 14(1), 17(7) and (8) TEU. It is worth recalling in this respect the words of J. Monnet, President of the High Authority, addressing the ECSC Parliamentary Assembly: "The High Authority has been entrusted with the implementation of the

objectives laid down in the Treaty. It is to you, and to you only, that the High Authority is responsible." (see Debates in the Common Assembly - Session of 11 September 1952, Opening address to the Assembly concerning the High Authority's programmes, reported in European Parliament (2010:56). The Treaty (see Art. 17(7) TEU) sets a two-stage procedure for appointing the European Commission. The European Council shall propose to the European Parliament a candidate for President of the Commission. This candidate shall be elected by the European Parliament by a majority of its members. Failing this, the Council of Ministers must put forward another name who shall be elected by the European Parliament following the same procedure. Then, by common accord with the President-elect, the Council shall propose the other members of the Commission. The College of Commissioners must then be endorsed as a body by the European Parliament through a vote of consent. On the basis of this consent, the Commission shall be appointed by the European Council, acting by a qualified majority.

[41] See Art. 17(3) TEU. The Treaty stresses that in carrying out its responsibilities, the Commission shall be completely independent. Except for the common foreign, defence and security policies, its members "shall neither seek nor take instructions from any Government or other institution, body, office or entity" (see Arts 17(3) and 18(2) TEU). The Treaty also provides that member states shall respect the independence of the members of the Commission and "shall not seek to influence them in the performance of their tasks" (see Art. 245 TFEU).

[42] See European Commission (2002:25). It is interesting to note in this respect that the Treaty itself recognises that national interests might not be in line with European ones. Indeed, the Treaty states that members states "shall facilitate the achievement of the Union's tasks and refrain from any measure which could jeopardise the attainment of the Union's objectives" (see Art. 4(3) TEU). Similarly, concerning the common foreign and security policy, member states "shall refrain from any action which is contrary to the interests of the Union or likely to impair its effectiveness as a cohesive force in international relations" (see Art. 24(3) TEU). Also, member states "shall take the same measures to counter fraud affecting the financial interests of the Union as they take to counter fraud affecting their own financial interests" (see Art. 325(2) TFEU).

[43] See CEPS, EGMONT & EPC (2007: 23).

[44] The two concepts are discussed in Pisani (1956:324-325).

[45] See Auditor General of Canada (2002:12).

[46] For a complete review of the EU budget process, see European Commission (2008). For a critical analysis, see the numerous contributions presented in the context of the EU budget review (http://ec.europa.eu/budget/reform/index_en.htm).

[47] See Barroso (2008).

[48] See European Commission (2004:5, 8).

[49] It is worth mentioning that, already in 1978, the Commission had tried to define the intervention of the EU budget on the basis of criteria such as 'economies of scale', the 'need for a global approach with the other policies funded' or the 'reduction of the burden of national budgets' (see European Commission, 1978:6-8). However these criteria turned out to be too vague to be applied. With the Lisbon Treaty it would still be possible for the EU budget to intervene in all sectors. Indeed, while the Treaty establishes three types of categories and areas of EU competence (see note 18), it does not provide operational criteria to define the EU area of intervention.

[50] See European Commission (2002:20). For example, immigration, justice, taxation, the labour market, energy and telecommunications are all sectors in which responsibilities are still largely national but which doubtlessly have effects across frontiers.

[51] Gros (2008:2) argues that the current composition of spending is the result of historical accidents and that the main legacy of the 'founding' compromises on agriculture and Structural Funds is that the budget is basically seen as a vehicle for the redistribution of money between member states, rather than a tool for fostering common goals.

[52] Farmers receive an amount of money based approximately on the area they farm (regardless what they produce), provided that they comply with a number of agro-environmental requirements.

[53] One of the aims is to start a process of structural transformation of the economy, thus favouring the recovery of economic systems and the development of trade. In this respect, although in different circumstances and within a peculiar context, there are conceptual similarities with the post-Second World War European Recovery Program (also known as the Marshall Plan, 1948-1951) through which the United States of America channelled some €100 billion to 16 European states.

[54] According to the principle of additionality, EU transfers for Structural policies should not replace public or equivalent structural expenditure by a member state. As a general rule the level of the expenditure shall be at least equal to the amount of average annual expenditure in real terms attained during the previous programming period (see Art. 15(1) of Regulation No 1083/2006 of the European Parliament and of the Council, as amended by Regulation No. 539/2010, 16.6.2010, OJ L 158 of 24.6.2010).

[55] As defined by Danuta Hübner (2007a:3), the former European Commissioner responsible for Regional Policy.

---

56 See European Commission (1977:17). One should observe that the funds available are usually not fully used (for example, a surplus of €2.25 billion, amounting to 1.9% of the budget, was recorded in 2009). One reason is the slow process of disbursing the funds for operations co-financed by member states (thus depending to a large extent upon their administrative capacity to set up and implement projects) and managed over a number of years, e.g. Cohesion Policy.

57 BusinessDictionary.com defines public goods as: "Item whose consumption is not decided by the individual consumer but by the society as a whole, and which is financed by taxation. A public good (or service) may be consumed without reducing the amount available for others, and cannot be withheld from who do not pay for it. Public goods (and services) include economic statistics and other information, law-and-order enforcement, national defence, national parks, etc. No market exists for such goods, and they must be provided to everyone by the government."

58 See European Commission (2006:20).

59 See Art. 312(1) TFEU. For a review of the features of the financial framework, see Cipriani (2007), in particular the section on "Financial perspective': Whose perspective?", p. 4.

60 See European Council, Financial Perspective 2007-2013, 15915/05, Brussels, 19 December 2005, p. 1.

61 Member states hold the 'purse strings'. This is the consequence of the respective powers of the two arms of the EU budgetary authority (the European Parliament and the Council) outlined by Art. 314(10) TFEU. The legal framework for EU revenue is provided by the Own resources Decision (for the period 2007–13, the Council's Decision 2007/436/EC, Euratom of 7 June 2007 on the system of the European Communities' own resources, OJ L 163, 23.6.2007). The Own Resources Decision establishes in particular the global ceiling on EU revenue, the typology of the resources financing the budget and the burden-sharing arrangements among member states. The Decision, on which the European Parliament can only give an opinion, has first to be unanimously adopted by the EU Council of Ministers and, to come into force, requires ratification by all member states according to their own constitutional rules (see Art. 311 TFEU). Hence, the Own Resources Decision constitutes in practice a treaty within the EU Treaty.

62 Member states have traditionally taken the stance of accepting a revision of the financial framework subject to not increasing the overall spending. Therefore any increase in a ceiling had to be compensated by a corresponding decrease of another ceiling. It is worth mentioning in this respect the difficulties faced by two major EU projects in obtaining the necessary funding. The first example is provided by the European satellite radio-navigation programmes (EGNOS and Galileo). Owing to

the failed negotiations with the private consortium, which had initially been expected to secure at least two-thirds of the financing for the deployment phase, the project had to face a funding gap of €2.4 billion for 2008–12 (while only €1 billion was provided for by the financial perspective 2007-13). Member states opposed an increase of the overall budgetary ceiling and only agreed a redeployment of existing funds, mostly from unused agricultural spending and other budget lines. A similar case is provided by ITER, an international collaborative project involving seven partners (the EU, China, India, Japan, Russia, South Korea and the United States of America) for a planned duration of 35 years. The Commission announced in May 2010 that the project was facing substantial overall cost increases, more than doubling the EU's share of the costs (from the initial €2.7 billion to around €7.2 billion). In particular, the shortfall for the remaining period (2012-13) of the current financial framework is about €1.4 billion. As member states were not prepared to follow the Commission's initial proposal to either raise the EU budget spending ceiling or have member states provide direct contributions (see COM (2010) 226, 4.5.2010 and MEMO/10/165, 5.5.2010), a kind of *déjà vu* plan in the Galileo project has been envisaged, redeploying €460 million from the 7th Framework Programme for Research and recycling unused funds in the current framework programme (see the Commission's press release IP/10/988 of 20.7.2010). Parliament, whose backing is necessary to adopt the Commission's proposal, has however opposed the redeployment of funds within the 7th Framework Programme for Research (see Parliament resolution of 20.10.2010 on Council's position on draft general budget of the European Union for the financial year 2011, para. 24). A solution for the ITER financing is still pending as of 15 November 2010.

[63] The EU budget is financed from three main sources of revenue. The first of these are customs duties, levied at the external frontiers of the EU at rates based on the Common Customs Tariff, and sugar levies paid by sugar producers to finance the export refunds for sugar. The second source of revenue is represented by the Value Added Tax (VAT) own resource, which is levied on member states' statistical 'notional' harmonised VAT bases, calculated on the basis of national VAT receipts. The third resource, levied at a uniform rate in proportion to the Gross National Income (GNI) of each member state, is a residual resource used to balance the budget. The EU budget is always assured of sufficient revenue; Art. 310(1) TFEU provides that revenue and expenditure must be in balance. The VAT-based and GNI-based resources are no more than a financial contribution calculated according to different parameters. For a critical analysis of the EU budget financing, see Cipriani (2007), especially the chapter "Reads as 'Own Resources', Means National Contributions", p. 42.

[64] The term 'budgetary balances' refers to the accounting balance between the contributions that the member states pay into the EU budget and the EU expenditure in favour of beneficiaries resident in their territory. Such calculations are traditionally a key element of the decision-making process of the Union. A widespread conventional milestone of this tendency is the declaration of Mrs Thatcher, the then British Prime Minister, at the Dublin European Council in November 1979: "We are not asking the Community or anyone else for money. We are simply asking for our own money back."

[65] See Barroso (2009:35-36). Gros (2008:2) stresses that this means that in the inter-governmental negotiations that determine the budget, no voice will defend overall EU interests. In face of an EU-wide, encompassing interest, member states would tend to favour choices leading to more money for them, even if at a lower overall efficiency. Among the numerous 'corrective mechanisms' one should recall the UK rebate (which limits the balance between UK payments to the EU budget and EU expenditure in its favour to one-third), the variable financing of this rebate according to the member states concerned (Germany, Austria, the Netherlands and Sweden pay only 25% of their normal share), the limitation of the VAT resource calculation base to 50% of GNI, the reduction of the rate of call of the VAT resource for some member states (Austria, Germany, the Netherlands and Sweden), the member states' levy of 25% of customs duties collected and ad hoc 'bonuses' for several member states. For a critical analysis of the different arrangements applied to the revenue side and the concept of budgetary balances, see Cipriani (2007), namely the chapters "Exception as the Rule, to Each his Own" and "Budgetary Balances - An Irresistible Temptation", p. 65 and 88.

[66] See European Parliament, Resolution of 8 June 2005 on Policy Challenges and Budgetary Means of the Enlarged Union 2007–13, para. L.

[67] In 2009, member states' contributions (VAT + GNI resources) have represented 0.73% of the EU GNI. This corresponds to a per-capita average contribution of € 189 (with two extremes, €39 and €469 respectively for residents of Bulgaria and Luxembourg). When adding up other EU revenue (customs duties and sugar levies) this average raises to €217.

[68] See European Commission (1998, annex 2, p. 3). Gros (2008:2) observes that European citizens have no clear perception of the total cost of the Union and the overall benefits of common action financed by the budget. But the few direct beneficiaries (mainly farmers) are well aware of budgetary transfers in their favour and place pressure on their government to preserve them indefinitely. The relative lack of knowledge among citizens concerning the European Union budget is confirmed by a survey by Eurobarometer. Only one in ten Europeans knows about the European Union budget (10%), half of them have heard of it but do not really

know what it involves (51%) and, finally, a third have never heard of it (33%). It is also interesting to note that respondents in the oldest EU member states are more likely not to have heard of the European Union budget: 36% versus 25% of the countries having joined since 2004 (see European Commission, 2010:207-208).

[69] In its 2004 own resources report (see European Commission, Financing the European Union, Commission report on the operation of the own resources system, Vol. II, COM(2004) 505 final, Brussels, 14 July 2004, p. 54), the Commission made a proposal for a genuinely fiscal resource, based on VAT which is the sole European tax for which the base harmonisation is quite advanced. The idea implied that as part of the national VAT rate paid by taxpayers there will be an EU rate, to be levied for the benefit of the EU budget. Citizens would not have to support an additional tax burden as the EU rate would be offset by an equivalent decrease of the national VAT rate. For visibility purposes, the EU VAT and national VAT should appear as separate taxes on the invoice or receipt that a taxable person provides to the customer.

[70] See Art. 1 TEU. The origin of this expression goes back to both the Treaties of Maastricht (1992) and Amsterdam (1997) which introduced the notion of 'openness'. It is worth recalling that, with the Declaration of European Council of Laeken (14-15 December 2001), the member states had already taken note that "the European Union institutions must be brought closer to its citizens". On that occasion, the member states recognised that European citizens do not always see the connection between the Union's major objectives and its daily work and, more importantly, "they feel that deals are all too often cut out of their sight and they want better democratic scrutiny" (Document SN 300/1/01 REV 1, p. 20).

[71] See European Parliament, Resolution of 12 July 2007 on the role and effectiveness of Cohesion policy in reducing disparities in the poorest regions of the EU, point P.

[72] The option to finance the EU budget by a real fiscal resource has been regularly discussed since the early days of the founding Treaties, which foresaw the possibility of replacing member states' contributions by own resources (see Art. 201 of the 1957 EEC Treaty). Many proposals have been made but none has found yet the required unanimous support (for a review of possible tax-based EU own resources see Cattoir (2004)). In 1965, the Commission proposed to allow the European Parliament (once directly elected) to create independent sources of revenue for the Community (see European Commission, 1965). Among others, the issue has been examined by the study group on the role of public finance in European integration chaired by D. MacDougal (European Commission, 1977) and by the Reflection Group for preparing the 1996 Intergovernmental Conference chaired by C. Westendorp. Following the Council request of December 2005 to carry out a comprehensive reassessment of the financial framework, the

Commission has initiated a review of the EU budget. The starting point was the adoption of the public consultation document "Reforming the Budget, Changing Europe" (see SEC(2007) 1188 final, 12.9.2007). The consultation process aimed at providing the means for reflecting on changes needed on spending and income (for a summary of contributions see SEC(2008)2739, 3.11.2008). As a result of this process, the European Commission presented in October 2010 its conclusions on the budget review and its views on the main priorities for the EU budget in the coming years. This includes several options for a new source of tax revenue, like an EU taxation of the financial sector, EU revenues from auctioning under the greenhouse gas Emissions Trading System, a EU charge related to air transport, a EU VAT, a EU energy tax and a EU corporate income tax (see COM (2010) 700, 19.10.2010, p. 27). As indicated by President Barroso, it is not a question of an EU tax but of finding new sources of financing to gradually replace member states contributions (see Statement of President Barroso on the budget review, 19 October 2010 http://ec.europa.eu/commission_2010-2014/president/pdf/statement_en.pdf).

73 Opposition to a VAT-based resource has often also been founded on the traditional view that this indirect tax is inherently regressive because its assessment base is structurally higher in the least prosperous member states than it is in the richest ones. However, some authors are not convinced that the regressivity of VAT is a real issue. For example, Begg, Grimwade & Price (1997:10), and Gretschmann (1998:25-26) challenge the opinion that the VAT resource has a significant regressive effect. Gros (2008:8, 11) observes that available data indicate that among countries with high VAT revenues, one finds both rich (Sweden) and poor (Hungary); the same applies to countries with low VAT revenues in proportion to GDP (e.g. Spain, a Cohesion country, and Italy, with GDP per capita above the EU average).

74 See note 69.

75 One may notice in this respect that when looking at possible new funding sources for the EU budget, one of the criteria put forward by the Commission is that, if feasible, the proceeds of a new resource should be collected directly by the EU outside national budgets (see COM (2010) 700, op. cit, p. 27). This would represent a significant change compared to the present situation where EU revenue is collected by member states' administrations.

76 Parliament has recently stressed the need for a stronger and increased degree of flexibility and a simplification of the procedure for shifting resources between the different headings of the multi-annual financial framework (see European Parliament, Resolution of 22 September 2010 on the proposal for a Council regulation laying down the multi-annual financial framework for the years 2007-

2013, point xv). The Commission's budget review paper recognises the need for greater flexibility in the use of available appropriations (see COM (2010) 700, op. cit., point 4.7, p. 23).

[77] Reference is made here to EU expenditure for Agriculture, Rural Development, Fisheries and Structural actions which, de facto or explicitly, is pre-allocated by member state at the time of the multi-annual financial framework's approval. It has been estimated that over 90% of the EU budget goes to funding EU policies and activities that have been agreed by all the member states (see European Commission, Annual accounts of the European Union, Financial Year 2009, SEC(2010) 963, 20.7.2010, p. 4).

[78] The 2010 budget authorises expenditure for €123 billion (payment appropriations). The revenues needed to finance the budget account for 0.99% of the total GNI. This compares with a ceiling of 1.23% of GNI as the limit for EU expenditure.

[79] See Art. 49(1) of the Financial Regulation, Council Regulation (EC, Euratom) No 1605/2002, op. cit. Following entering into force of the Treaty of Lisbon almost all EU legislation will be endorsed by both the Parliament and Council (see also note 30).

[80] 'Eligibility rules' designate a set of legal requirements, stemming from EU and national legislation, defining the conditions for national expenditure to be reimbursed by the EU budget. These rules govern in particular the location and range of the activities, the cost categories and the period during which expenditure can be incurred. There are a number of additional conditions for expenditure to be eligible, for example the compliance with EU rules and policies (such as public procurement, competition, environment; adequate publicity of the operations funded; costs actually borne by the beneficiary; retention of supporting documents and keeping investments in operation for a certain period). The EU budget reimburses the full costs of the income support to farmers (as well as of measures to regulate agricultural markets), while for Cohesion policy (as well as for other funding such as the European Agricultural Fund for Rural Development and the European Fisheries Fund) co-financing is applied and thus part of the costs rest with national budgets. Co-financing is a key principle for EU grants (see Art. 109(1) of the Financial Regulation No 1605/2002, op. cit.). It also represents an "indirect" assurance for 'net-payers' member states for effective spending and mitigating deadweight. For example, the around €344 billion of EU funds for the Cohesion policy are closely linked to the €144 billion of national co-financing. This means that for every €10 of EU expenditure in this area, another €4 are spent (on average) by the national budgets.

---

[81] For an overview of the different programmes funded by the EU budget, see Statement of estimates of the European Commission for the Financial year 2011, Financial programming 2011 - 2013, SEC(2010)473, p. 116, May 2010, available at http://ec.europa.eu/budget/library/documents/annual_budgets_reports_accounts/2011/2011_Draft_budg_preparation_en.pdf. See also later Table 1.

[82] This is also the case for the agricultural policy, which is commonly thought to be financed exclusively by the EU budget. Actually, as it has been observed (S. Tarditi - Tutto quello che non sappiamo della PAC, available at http://www.lavoce.info/articoli/pagina1897.html), the national budgets continue to finance the agricultural sector in various ways and at a significant level. Indeed, agriculture is considered in the EU Treaty to be a shared competence (see Art. 4(2) TEU).

[83] See Arts 17(1) TEU and 317 TFEU. One should mention that the provision for the Commission to "manage programmes" is an addition of the Lisbon Treaty. The definition of "manage" is "to be in charge of, to administer" (Collins); "to direct or carry on business or affairs" (Merriam-Webster). A synonym for "manage" is "conduct" (Merriam-Webster) or "to handle" (Online etymology dictionary). This addition in the Treaty seems to indicate an enhancement of the Commission's role, further confirmed by other linguistic versions of the Treaty (DE, *"Sie führt den Haushaltsplan aus und verwaltet die Programme"*; ES, *"Ejecutará el presupuesto y gestionará los programas"*; FR, *"Elle exécute le budget et gère les programmes"*; IT, *"Dà esecuzione al bilancio e gestisce i programmi"*). One should also note that, unlike Arts 14 and 16 TEU where the Treaty on European Union expressly indicates that legislative and budgetary functions are a shared competence of Parliament and Council, Art. 17(1) TEU does not mention the cooperation with the member states in the EU budget. This expression is only indicated in Art. 317 TFEU about the budgetary implementation. This seems to confirm that such cooperation refers to specific implementation tasks only. It therefore does not undermine the Commission's full responsibility.

[84] This expression has been added to the previous Art. 274 of the Treaty establishing the European Community (TEC) by the Treaty of Lisbon (Art. 317 TFEU). The origin of this addition are the works of the European Convention (2002-2003) where the Commission had proposed "to examine the feasibility of sharing responsibility for budget implementation when the member states are responsible for most of the management of funds" (see European Commission, Communication on a Project for the European Union, COM(2002) 247 final, Brussels, 22 May 2002, p. 6). The Treaty of Lisbon has however confirmed the Commission's ultimate responsibility (see also note 107).

[85] The Financial Regulation defines the rules which determine in particular the procedure to be adopted for establishing and implementing the budget and for presenting and auditing accounts. It also provides for checks on the responsibility of financial actors, in particular authorising officers and accounting officers (see Art. 322(1) TFEU). Before the recent entering into force of the Treaty on the functioning of the European Union, the adoption of the Financial Regulation was a sole Council competence. This competence is now shared with the European Parliament, both institutions having the same degree of lawmaking power.

[86] See note 19 and Box 1 "The principles of subsidiarity and proportionality".

[87] Where the Commission implements the budget on a centralised basis, implementation tasks shall be performed either directly by its departments or indirectly, through "executive agencies", EU bodies (such as the European Investment Bank or the European Investment Fund), national or international bodies with a public-service mission. Centralised management by the Commission is limited mainly to fields like Research, Information society, Education & Culture, Transport & Energy and some external actions.

[88] This concerns mostly EU humanitarian and development programmes aid implemented by an international organisation (e.g. United Nations and its agencies, World Bank, Red Cross) through contribution agreements. Nuclear decommissioning funds are subject to joint management with the European Bank for Reconstruction and Development (EBRD).

[89] This refers mainly to Agriculture and Cohesion policy. The same arrangements also apply to other spending programmes like the European Refugee Fund, the European Return Fund and the Solidarity Fund. Concerning third countries, financial assistance involves in particular support to countries candidate to EU membership and economic and development assistance in various regions of the world.

[90] This is normally provided in the basic act establishing a spending programme. However, the Financial Regulation itself (see Art. 53b(1) of Council Regulation (EC, Euratom) No 1605/2002, op. cit.) prescribes that "shared management" shall apply in particular to the actions referred to the European agricultural guarantee fund, Structural funds, Cohesion fund, European fisheries Fund, and European agricultural fund for Rural development. It provides further that "[w]here the Commission implements the budget by shared management, implementation tasks shall be delegated to Member States".

[91] It should also be noted that the possibility for the Commission to delegate its executive powers to third parties is strictly defined and limited. This is only foreseen in centralised management (delegation to executive agencies) and decentralised management (delegation to third country, national or international

public-sector bodies) (see Art. 54 of the Financial Regulation, Council Regulation (EC, Euratom) No 1605/2002, op. cit.).

92 Among the EU requirements one may note for example, the separation of duties between management, payment and control functions; the establishment of proper accounting systems; the definition of powers and responsibilities of the financial actors; the modalities and intensity of checks to be performed; the implementing procedures (competitive tendering, State aid rules). The accreditation of national bodies is a member states' competence, although subject to EU requirements.

93 To ensure that the funds are used in accordance with the applicable rules and principles, member states shall take all the legislative, regulatory and administrative or other measures necessary for protecting the EU financial interests. To this effect they shall in particular "(a) satisfy themselves that actions financed from the budget are actually carried out and to ensure that they are implemented correctly; (b) prevent and deal with irregularities and fraud; (c) recover funds wrongly paid or incorrectly used or funds lost as a result of irregularities or errors; (d) ensure, by means of relevant sector-specific regulations (...) adequate annual *ex-post* publication of beneficiaries of funds deriving from the budget. To that effect, the Member States shall conduct checks and shall put in place an effective and efficient internal control system (...) [and] "shall bring legal proceedings as necessary and appropriate". Member states' control of final beneficiaries implies both 100% administrative checks and on-the-spot checks (normally of at least 5% annually).

94 See Box 2 "An overview of the EU's financial frameworks".

95 Protocol No. 25 on the exercise of shared competence (Treaty of Lisbon) clarifies that "when the Union has taken action in a certain area, the scope of this exercise of competence only covers those elements governed by the Union act in question and therefore does not cover the whole area".

96 Contrary to "shared management", the degree of "decentralisation" depends on the Commission's assurance on the management and control systems in place. This determines whether also payments are decentralised and whether control by the Commission on procurement takes place ex-ante or only ex-post. In the lowest level of decentralisation, the Commission entrusts to the country's administration the tendering and contracting process, while keeping control on all decisions ex-ante and making payments directly to the contractors. In the case of pre-accession countries, national administrations charged of budgetary tasks, whose organisational structure is subject to a number of binding conditions, go through a process of accreditation by the Commission. Payments to the contractors are made by the national administrations which then claim back the funds from the Commission. The latter monitors the implementation on an ongoing basis. In some

cases where national administrations meet more stringent management and control requirements, the ex-ante control over procurement may be removed by the Commission.

97 The Seventh Framework Programme (FP7) is the EU's main instrument for funding research in Europe in selected priority areas, with a total budget of over €50 billion for 2007-13. Projects are given, in general, a grant contributing a certain percentage to the overall costs. EU funded activities are implemented by a large number of public and private entities in different member states or associated states. Beneficiaries may be research institutes, companies, public administrations, experienced researchers, organisations and researchers from third countries. The beneficiaries or partners usually work as a consortium across member states or associated states.

98 Comitology goes back to the 1960s, where the first management committee was created in the framework of the agricultural markets. But a formal provision has been inserted in the treaties only in February 1986 following adoption of the Single European Act. Art. 202 TEC envisaged the possibility of the Council conferring on the Commission "in the acts which the Council adopts, powers for the implementation of the rules which the Council lays down". The spirit of this provision is that implementing measures are a full part of the powers of the EU legislative body (at the time the Council alone), which are delegated to the Commission for reasons of convenience. The Council could thus "impose certain requirements in respect of the exercise of these powers" and it could "reserve the right, in specific cases, to exercise directly implementing powers itself". Council Decision No. 1999/468/EC of 28 June 1999 (OJ L 184, 17.7.1999, pp. 23-26), lastly amended by Council Decision No 2006/512/EC of 17 July 2006 (OJ L 200, 22.7.2006, pp. 11–13) provided for five different procedures (Advisory procedure, Management procedure, Regulatory procedure, Regulatory procedure with scrutiny and Safeguard procedure). End 2009, there were 266 committees, mostly in the fields of Transport and Energy, Environment, Enterprises and Agriculture. More than one-hundred of them were operating under the management procedure which is relevant for the EU budget implementation. Under the management procedure the Commission submits to the committee a draft of the measures to be taken on which the committee shall deliver its opinion. The Commission may in theory adopt the measures immediately, also in the absence of an opinion (no quorum for a favourable, nor for an unfavourable opinion as a result of the vote in the committee) or even in case of an unfavourable opinion. However, following a committee's negative opinion, these measures are submitted to the Council that may take a different decision within a period of a maximum of three months acting by qualified majority. In the meantime the Commission may defer application of the measures decided. By establishing a distinction between 'delegated acts' and

'implementing acts' the Treaty of Lisbon substantially modifies the framework for implementing powers that are conferred upon the Commission by the EU legislator (see note 104). This requires in particular the setting of new rules and general principles concerning mechanisms for control by member states of the Commission's exercise of implementing powers. The Commission's proposal (see COM (2010) 83, 9.3.2010) maintains the previous Committee structure, but envisages only two procedures compared to five before. Are foreseen the advisory procedure (as the general rule) and a new "examination" procedure which would replace the existing management and regulatory procedures. It should finally be noted that on the basis of the *acquis communautaire*, legislation adopted before the entry into force of the Treaty of Lisbon continues to be applied, including all provisions on comitology, until the basic act is repealed or modified.

[99] In this respect one may notice that in a declaration to Council Decision No. 1999/468/EC, op. cit., the Commission recalled that under the management procedure "its constant practice is to try to secure a satisfactory decision which will also muster the widest possible support within the Committee. The Commission will take account of the position of the members of the Committee and act in such a way as to avoid going against any predominant position which might emerge against the appropriateness of an implementing measure."

[100] For example, the "Committee of Independent Experts", convened early 1999 under the auspices of the Parliament and the Commission to examine the Commission management practices, regretted "that a system which should introduce transparency and accountability into the management of programmes in fact can remove responsibility from the Commission for the management decisions taken. Commission managers can (and do) point to the extraneous demands of Member States as justification for management decisions which cannot be justified according to objective financial criteria" (see Committee of Independent Experts, Second Report on Reform of the Commission: Analysis of current practice and proposals for tackling mismanagement, irregularities and fraud, 10 September 1999, Vol. II, point 7.15.14, p. 136).

[101] It is worth mentioning that the intervention of "comitology" procedures in the budget implementation has been the subject of institutional disputes. In particular, the Commission and the European Parliament have criticised the negative effects of these procedures on the institutional balance and the separation of powers, the opacity, the unjustified delays and the pointless costs. The Court of Justice had nevertheless considered that the mechanism of a management committee was not likely to distort the Community structure and institutional balance and that this procedure was one of the methods to which the Council could legitimately subordinate authorisation to the Commission (see Case-law 25-70, Einfuhr- und Vorratsstelle für Getreide und Futtermittel v Köster and Berodt & Co. Judgment of

the Court 17.12.1970, ECR 1970, p. 1161). Concerning in particular the implementation of the EU budget, the Commission argued that the intervention of a management committee was likely to encroach on its exclusive responsibility as regards budgetary implementation. Indeed, the Council could ultimately have taken a different decision, which nevertheless would have involved the use of budget appropriations. In addition, any decision which would have interfered with this exclusive responsibility of the Commission would at the same time have deprived the European Parliament of its supervisory powers in respect of the implementation of the budget. It was on this basis that the Commission decided to take the Council to the European Court of Justice. The Court judged however that the adoption by the Council of acts that are individual in scope, with financial consequences, which it then authorises the Commission to implement, does not prejudice the Commission's power to implement the budget on its own responsibility (see Case-law 16/88, Commission of the European Communities v Council of the European Communities. Judgment of the Court of 24 October 1989, ECR 1989, p. 3457, points 16-17). In this way, the implementation of the budget was interpreted by the Court of Justice as being on an equal footing with any other implementation power conferred by the Council on the Commission. In so doing, the Court identified the pre-eminence of the general rules enacted by Arts 202 and 211 TEC and did not find that Art. 274 TEC constituted an example of a *lex specialis*.

[102] See European Commission (2001:31).

[103] See European Commission, Communication of the Commission on the institutional architecture, COM(2002) 728, 11 December 2002, p. 13. See also European Convention, Proposal from the Commission's representative in the Working group to distinguish legislative and executive functions in the institutional system of the European Union, working group IX, working document No. 16, 7.11.2002.

[104] The Treaty of Lisbon establishes a hierarchy of norms with a distinction between legislative acts (regulations, directives, decisions, Arts 288-289 TFEU), delegated acts (the Commission to adopt delegated acts in the field of competence of the European Parliament and/or the Council, Art. 290 TFEU) and implementing acts (acts adopted by the Commission in its own field of competence, Art. 291 TFEU). As observed by the Commission, the distinction between "quasi-legislative measures" which are referred to as "delegated acts" and "implementing" or executive acts, which is mutually exclusive and did not exist in the previous EC Treaty (see Art. 202 TEC), originate from the different scope of the two provisions. When it receives the power to adopt "delegated acts" under Art. 290 TFEU, the Commission is authorised to supplement or amend certain non-essential elements of the legislative acts in the interests of efficiency, taking measures that the legislator could have adopted itself. In this respect Art. 290 TFEU clarifies that

"[t]he objectives, content, scope and duration of the delegation of power shall be explicitly defined in the legislative acts. The essential elements of an area shall be reserved for the legislative act and accordingly shall not be the subject of a delegation of power". It provides further that "[l]egislative acts shall explicitly lay down the conditions to which the delegation is subject". Such a delegation is always discretionary and the legislator may control the exercise of the Commission's powers by means of a right of revocation and/or a right of objection. The situation is rather different concerning the implementation of EU binding acts which, according to Art. 291 TFEU, would normally be the prerogative of the member states, as a consequence of the increased focus put on the subsidiarity principle by the Treaty of Lisbon and the consequent decentralised implementation. The Commission is given implementing powers only where such acts require uniform implementing conditions. However, these powers do not imply the exercise of any 'quasi-legislative' power and they are purely executive. This is why it is the member states (and they alone, not the EU legislator - Parliament and Council) that are responsible for controlling the Commission's exercise of these implementing powers (see European Commission, Communication to the European Parliament and the Council, Implementation of Art. 290 of the Treaty on the Functioning of the European Union, COM (2009) 673, 9.12.2009, point 2.2; and Proposal for a Regulation of the European Parliament and of the Council laying down the rules and general principles concerning mechanisms for control by member states of the Commission's exercise of implementing powers, COM (2010) 83, 9.3.2010, point 1).

[105] Communication of the Commission on the institutional architecture, COM(2002) 728, op. cit., p. 14.

[106] These bodies are not less than two thousand in Agriculture and Structural policies alone. Also, there are about 12 million full-time farmers in the 27 EU countries who may potentially benefit from the CAP subsidies. For Rural development alone (Pillar 2 of the Common Agricultural Policy) the total number of beneficiaries in 2008 was some 3.6 million. Structural policies co-finance about two million of projects and the current European Social Fund (ESF) programmes support 9 million people each year.

[107] See Arts 17(1) TEU and 317 TFEU. As in previous Treaty's amendments of the budgetary provisions (Treaties of Maastricht, 1992, and Amsterdam, 1997), the Treaty of Lisbon has confirmed the Commission's ultimate responsibility by stating that it shall implement the budget "on its own responsibility" and "having regard to the principles of sound financial management". To this effect, the Commission should count on adequate cooperation from member states, with the latter having control and audit obligations in the implementation of the budget and resulting responsibilities (see Art. 317 TFEU). The Commission's ultimate

responsibility in the budget implementation is also enounced in Art. 48 of the Financial Regulation, Council Regulation (EC, Euratom) No 1605/2002, op. cit. Several judgments of the European Court of Justice have confirmed this interpretation (see for example Case-law 16/88, Commission/Council, op. cit., point 15; Case-law C-106/96, United Kingdom of Great Britain and Northern Ireland v Commission of the European Communities. Judgment of the Court 12 May 1998, ECR I-2729, point 21).

108 The Treaty of Lisbon has formally recognised that the budget shall be implemented "in cooperation with the Member States" (see Art. 317 TFEU). The "cooperation with the member states" is nothing more than the consequence of Art. 4(3) TEU which indicates that the Union and the member states shall assist each other in carrying out tasks which flow from the Treaties. Member states shall take any appropriate measure to ensure fulfilment of their obligations and shall facilitate the achievement of the Union's tasks.

109 See European Commission, Synthesis of Annual Activity Reports 2003 of DGs and Services, COM (2004) 418, 9.6.2004, p. 11.

110 Reference is made to the institutional crisis that lead to the resignation of the Santer Commission in March 1999 (for the context see Cipriani (2007), in particular the section "The need for a management culture", p. 106).

111 See European Commission, The control system for Cohesion Policy, How it works in the 2007–13 budget period, October 2009, p. 7. The Financial Regulation No 1605/2002, op. cit., Art. 28a(2) defines "internal control" as "a process applicable at all levels of the management and designed to provide reasonable assurance of achieving the following objectives:

(a) effectiveness, efficiency and economy of operations;

(b) reliability of reporting;

(c) safeguarding of assets and information;

(d) prevention and detection of fraud and irregularities;

(e) adequate management of the risks relating to the legality and regularity of the underlying transactions, taking into account the multiannual character of programmes as well as the nature of the payments concerned". Internal control is carried out by management and staff and is integrated into the internal structures and operating processes (for example a Commission's Directorate-General or a national management authority). Within the Commission a distinction should made with "Internal audit", which is independent from management. Its main task is to perform independent assessments of management's internal control, risk management and governance, and provide recommendations for improvements. It can also supply consulting services. It is carried out by the Internal Audit Service

(IAS), a horizontal service that reports directly to the College. In addition, each service has an Internal Audit Capability (IAC) that reports directly to the Director General.

112 See note 93.

113 The difference between "interruption" and "suspension" constitutes a "subtlety" of the Cohesion policy legal framework (see Arts 91 and 92 of Regulation No 1083/2006, op. cit.). While "interruption" of payments is a decision taken by Directors-general and is limited to six months, "suspension" of payments has to be decided by the Commission. Funds cancellation may occur as a result of clearance procedures (see Art. 53(b)(4) of Council Regulation (EC, Euratom) No 1605/2002, op. cit).

114 For example the Commission has indicated that when it relies on other authorities to manage the risk of irregular spending, it "verifies the operation of this framework, and when it finds that EU funds have been put at excessive risk, it suspends payments and makes financial corrections, thus repairing the damage to the EU's budget" (see European Commission, A gap assessment between the internal control framework in the Commission Services and the control principles set out in the Court of Auditors' "proposal for a Community internal control framework" opinion No 2/2004, SEC(2005) 1152, 28.9.2005, p. 29). The same concept is expressed in the EU 2009 annual accounts (see SEC(2010) 963, 20.7.2010, p. 79).

115 Art. 287(1) TFEU stipulates that the Court of Auditors "shall provide the European Parliament and the Council with a statement of assurance as to the reliability of the accounts and the legality and regularity of the underlying transactions". An annual Statement of Assurance has been established for the first time concerning the financial year 1994. Since then the Court has not been in a position to confirm that the EU budget expenditure as a whole was legal and regular in all material aspects. The origin of this provision is to be found in a late stage in the drafting of the Maastricht Treaty (1992), with strong backing from the governments of the United Kingdom and the Netherlands and the support of the European Parliament's Budgetary Control Committee. The main objectives of the Statement of Assurance are to inform the discharge authority of whether:

- the consolidated financial statements of the general budget of the European Union present a true and fair view of the financial activities for the year and of the year-end situation; and
- legal and contractual provisions have been respected when executing the budget.

According to international standards auditors can give the following kinds of opinions:

- an *unqualified opinion* (also called "clean") when there is evidence that the accounts are reliable or the underlying transactions are legal and regular in all material aspects;
- an *adverse opinion* when the level of error in the underlying transactions is material and pervasive, or the accounts are not reliable;
- a *disclaimer of opinion* if auditors are unable to obtain sufficient appropriate audit evidence on which to base an opinion, and the possible effects are both material and pervasive;
- a *qualified opinion* when an unqualified opinion cannot be expressed but the effect of any disagreement or limitation on scope is not so pervasive as to require an adverse opinion or a disclaimer of opinion (see European Court of Auditors, The DAS methodology, available at http://eca.europa.eu/portal/pls/portal/docs/1/1671539.PDF).

116 The wording "irregularity" refers to misapplication or misunderstanding of the often complex rules of EU expenditure schemes. Payments are legal and regular when these conditions as well as the accuracy and existence of the underlying activities and/or costs are met, and the right beneficiaries receive the right amounts at the right time. An irregularity is not *per se* a fraud, which would imply that EU funds have intentionally been improperly claimed.

117 See European Commission, Communication from the President in agreement with Vice-President Wallström, Strategic Objectives 2005–2009, Europe 2010: A Partnership for European Renewal, Prosperity, Solidarity and Security, COM(2005) 12 final, 26.1.2005, p. 5. This objective has been reconfirmed for the current mandate (see Commissioner Šemeta's speech on 2008 Discharge before the European Parliament, 21 April 2010, SPEECH/10/2010, available at http://europa.eu/rapid/pressReleasesAction.do?reference=SPEECH/10/210).

118 In the Cohesion policy to €1 of EU spending corresponds on average €0.4 of national co-financing.

119 For the ERDF and the Cohesion Fund, over a third of the irregularities uncovered is connected to breaches of rules on public procurement (see the speech by Mrs. Hübner of 25 February 2008 before the European Parliament's Committee on Budgetary Control, document SPEECH/08/100). Total public procurement in the EU - i.e. the purchases of goods, services and public works by governments and public utilities - is estimated at about 16% of the Union's GDP or €1.500 billion in 2002. Undoubtedly the award of public contracts is a key factor for achieving the internal market, of the highest importance for public authorities. This high rate of irregularities for legislation put in place many years ago (some of the existing public procurement Directives date back to the 1970s) suggests that at least in some

cases the reason for such irregularities is a conflict of interests between the EU and the national level.

120 In its annual report on the implementation of the 2009 budget (see European Court of Auditors, 9.9.2010, http://eca.europa.eu/portal/pls/portal/docs/1/5926723.PDF) the Court of Auditors points out that although for the budget as a whole its estimate of error has fallen over recent years, EU payments continue to be materially affected by error except in two areas of expenditure ('Economic and financial affairs' and Administrative and other expenditure'). This is because supervisory and control systems are partially effective in preventing or detecting and correcting the reimbursement of overstated or ineligible costs. The Court observes however that its estimate of the most likely error in Cohesion spending was significantly lower in 2009 than in previous years (at least 3% of the expenditure certified by member states to the Commission should not have been reimbursed against 11 % for 2007 and 2008); though it remains the policy group most affected by error (36 % of payments to projects were affected by error). One should note in this connection that in 2009 the Commission has carried out an audit to assess the legality and regularity of Cohesion policy expenditure declarations for the period 2007-13, by applying an approach similar to the Court. The results of this examination indicated a rate of irregularity of around 5%, thus showing improvement compared to the past. However, it should be pointed out that the expenditure audited concerns systems covering only ten member states (namely excluding big funds recipients) and was related to the initial endowment of financial instruments where the risk of error is low (see European Commission, Impact of the action plan to strengthen the Commission's supervisory role under shared management of structural actions, COM(2010) 52, 18.2.2010, point 2.1, p. 11).

121 See European Commission, Protection of the European Union's financial interests, Fight against fraud Annual Report 2009, COM (2010) 382, 14.7.2010.

122 See European Commission, A gap assessment between the internal control framework in the Commission Services and the control principles set out in the Court of Auditors' "proposal for a Community internal control framework" opinion No 2/2004, SEC(2005) 1152, 28.9.2005, p. 23.

123 For a definition of "eligibility" rules see note 80.

124 For example, for Cohesion policies there are more than 200 pages of legal texts of EU legislation, without including other applicable provisions like for example those concerning the award of public contracts. Yet, it is still argued that EU regulatory requirements are not sufficiently clear or include gaps (see European Parliament, Study on Member State difficulties with Structural Funds management

and control systems in the programming period, doc. PE 411.278, 2 June 2010, pp. 1-2).

125 A recent study in the frame of Cohesion policy indicates that two-thirds of survey respondents consider that the focus on control requirements is no longer proportionate, it is deflecting managers' attention from content issues and it deters potential applicants for EU funds support, for example in the area of innovation (see European Parliament, Study on Member State difficulties with Structural Funds management and control systems in the programming period, op. cit., pp. 1-2). Bachtler & Mendez (2010:19) also report growing evidence that some organisations are discouraged from applying for funding.

126 The authors argue that the Commission's administrative reform programme in the aftermath of the EU's financial management and legitimacy crisis in the '90s has been the driver of an explosion in EU Cohesion policy auditing. This audit explosion corresponds to a compliance model, contrasting with the New Public Management ethos inspiring the Commission's reform programme. The ever-increasing attention given to financial management at both EU and national level has been at the expense of ensuring that programmes meet their policy objectives effectively.

127 "Simplification" is a recurrent issue. Several initiatives have been taken since the late 90's to simplify EU legislation. The latest initiative has been launched in 2007, with an Action Programme for Reducing Administrative Burdens in the European Union (in this context, the Commission appointed an High Level Group of Independent Stakeholders on Administrative Burdens, chaired by Mr Stoiber). The aim is to reduce administrative burdens on businesses arising from EU legislation by 25%. This is a joint target for both the EU and member states, covering EU legislation as well as national regulatory measures, and to be achieved by 2012 (see COM(2007) 23 final, 24.1.2007). The target has been endorsed by the European Council in March 2007 (see Presidency Conclusions, doc. 7224/1/07, REV 1, 2.5.2007, para. 24).

128 For example, in the Cohesion policy several measures were introduced like an increased use of lumps sums, standard scales of unit costs and indirect costs on a flat rate basis, wider acceptance of the use of national eligibility rules. The Commission has observed that for the final beneficiaries of Cohesion financial instruments the potential reduction linked to the simplification measures already adopted is calculated at 24% compared to the estimated administrative burden of complying with the requirements laid down for the previous programming period 2000-2006 (see DG "Regional policy" Annual Activity Report for the year 2009, 31.3.2010, p. 4, available at http://ec.europa.eu/atwork/synthesis/aar/doc/regio_aar.pdf).

---

[129] See Report from the Commission to the Council on the follow-up to 2007 Discharge Decisions (Summary) - Council Recommendations, COM(2009) 682, 10.12.2009, p. 4.

[130] See European Parliament resolution of 15 June 2010 on the mandate for the trilogue on the 2011 draft budget, para. 35.

[131] See Council recommendation in respect of the implementation of the budget for the financial year 2008, doc. 5826/10 Add 1, 3.2.2010, p. 6.

[132] See European Court of Auditors, Opinion No 1/2010 "Improving the financial management of the European Union budget: Risks and challenges", 14.1.2010, point 13.

[133] Art. 53b(4) of the Financial Regulation No. 1605/2002, op. cit., provides that in "shared management" arrangements, "[i]n order to ensure that the funds are used in accordance with the applicable rules, the Commission shall apply clearance-of-accounts procedures or financial correction mechanisms which enable it to assume final responsibility for the implementation of the budget". Art. 53c(2) contains a similar provision for the case of decentralised management, with third countries.

[134] It should be recalled that implementing competences of both the Commission and member states follow delegation by the EU legislator, i.e. there is no hierarchical primacy of the Commission over national bodies. See also note 7.

[135] See Art. 10(2) TEU.

[136] For example, the ex-post evaluation for the Cohesion policy 2000-06 remarks that no authorities were held accountable for not meeting the targets set (see European Commission (2010), *Ex-Post Evaluation of Cohesion Policy Programmes 2000-2006 financed by the European Regional Development Fund in Objective 1 and 2 Regions*, Synthesis Report, April, p. 11, http://ec.europa.eu/regional_policy/sources/docgener/evaluation/pdf/synthesis_eval2000_2006.pdf).

[137] See European Commission, Annual accounts of the European Communities, Financial Year 2009, SEC(2010) 963, 20.07.2010, p. 6. See also, European Commission, Governance Statement, 30 May 2007, points 1.1, 1.2, 3.1 and 3.2; and European Commission, Code of conduct for Commissioners, SEC (2004) 1487/2, 23.11.2004, section 2, p. 6.

[138] Art. 17(8) TEU states that "[t]he Commission, as a body, shall be responsible to the European Parliament". In contrast, the individual political responsibility of Commissioners has to be enforced by the Commission President who is therefore accountable to the European Parliament in this context. The Framework Agreement signed by Parliament and Commission on 20.10.2010 indicates that "[e]ach Member of the Commission shall take political responsibility for action in the field of which he or she is in charge, without prejudice to the principle of

Commission collegiality" (see Annex, Art. 4). And it provides also that "[i]f Parliament asks the President of the Commission to withdraw confidence in an individual Member of the Commission, he/she will seriously consider whether to request that Member to resign (...). The President shall either require the resignation of that Member or explain his/her refusal to do so before Parliament in the following part-session." (see Annex, Art. 5). Indeed, according to Art. 248 TFEU (whose origin is the Treaty of Nice, entered into force in February 2003), the President has the power to reallocate responsibilities to Members during the Commission's term of office. A Member of the Commission shall resign if the President so requests. The Treaty of Lisbon (Art. 17(6) TEU) has reinforced this provision by giving to the President full power in this respect (the approval of the College is not anymore necessary).

139 See Art. 17(7) TEU.

140 In addition to the statutory parliamentary committees, the Parliament may set up a temporary committee of inquiry to investigate alleged contraventions or maladministration in the implementation of Union law (Art. 226 TFEU). This faculty, introduced by the Maastricht Treaty (1992), is subject to the condition that the alleged facts are not being examined before a Court and the case is not still subject to legal proceedings. The *modus operandi* of a committee of inquiry is governed by the Decision 95/167/EC, Euratom, ECSC of the European Parliament, Council and Commission of 19 April 1995 (OJ L 113 of 19.5.95, p. 2) and by the Parliament's rules of procedure (Rule 185). The Parliament has used this possibility for the first time in 1996 to inquiry into the Community Transit Regime. Since then a committee of enquiry has been established in few other cases (to investigate alleged contraventions or maladministration in the implementation of Community law in relation to bovine spongiform encephalopathy - BSE, and to inquiry into the crisis of the Equitable Life Assurance Society). The establishment in 1999 of a "Committee of Independent Experts" has to be considered as a special case. The committee was convened under the auspices of the Parliament and the Commission (who agreed its composition and terms of reference), in the context of the institutional crisis of the end 90'. The Parliament made explicit that the committee had to report on their assessment in the first instance on the College of Commissioners (see European Parliament, Resolution of 14 January 1999 on improving the financial management of the Commission, para 1).

141 See Art. 318 TFEU.

142 The Parliament has stressed the need for a clearer definition of Commissioners' individual and collective political responsibility and accountability for their decisions and for the policy implementation by their services (see European Parliament, Resolution of 22 April 2008 on the discharge for implementation of the

European Union general budget for the financial year 2006, para. 73; and Resolution of 23 April 2009 on the discharge for implementation of the European Union general budget for the financial year 2007, para. 57). At hearings before the European Parliament of the Barroso II Commission, newly appointed Commissioners were asked questions like: "In what respect would you consider yourself responsible and accountable to the Parliament for your actions and for those of your departments?"). For a review of the political accountability in Europe, see Broeksteeg H., Van den Driessche, I., Verhey, L. (eds) (2008).

143 See European Commission, Synthesis of the Annual Activity Reports and declarations of the Directors-General and Heads of Service, COM (2002) 426, 24.7.2002, p. 10.

144 See European Commission, Synthesis of the Commission's management achievements in 2009, COM (2010) 281, 2.6.2010, p. 2.

145 European Commission, Governance Statement, 30 May 2007, point 3.2, p. 7.

146 European Council, Recommendation on the discharge to be given to the Commission in respect of the implementation of the budget for the financial year 2007, doc. 5587/09, ADD1/REV1, 4.2.2009, p. 10.

147 See European Parliament, Working document of Mrs I. Grässle on Governance in the European Commission, Part 1, doc. 392.252, 29.8.2007, p. 4.

148 See European Parliament, Resolution of 22 April 2008 with observations forming an integral part of the decision on discharge in respect of the implementation of the European Union general budget for the financial year 2006, section III - Commission, point 46.

149 In this respect, the Treaty seems to give ammo to such an interpretation when, in the context of the discharge procedure, it refers to the Commission's departments "which are responsible for the implementation of the budget" (see Art. 319(3) TFEU). The principle of the Institution's primary responsibility and the exercise of delegated responsibilities to authorising officers are set by Art. 59 of the Financial Regulation, Council Regulation (EC, Euratom) No 1605/2002, op. cit. This point has been stressed by the European Parliament in its discharge Resolution of 22 April 2008 concerning the financial year 2006 (para. 48; see also European Parliament, Working document of Mrs I. Grässle on Governance in the European Commission, Part 1, doc. 392.252, 29.8.2007, p. 4). For the background of the present responsibilities arrangements within the Commission, see European Commission: Supporting the reform of financial management : a new framework for authorising officers, SEC(2000) 2203, 13.12.2000; The annual reports and declarations required of Directors-General under the reform of the Commission, SEC (2001) 875, 27.6.2001; The 2002 review of the implementation of activity-based management in the Commission, including clarification of the methodology for the

establishment of Annual Activity Reports, COM(2003) 28, 21.1.2003; Clarification of the responsibilities of the key actors in the domain of internal audit and internal control in the Commission, SEC(2003) 59, 21.1.2003; Clarification of the role of Directors-General in the framework of shared management, C(2003)1830, 17.6.2003; Internal rules on the implementation of the general budget of the European Union, C(2010) 1858, 8.4.2010.

150 On that occasion the "Committee of Independent Experts" stressed that "[t]he separation between the political responsibility of Commissioners (for policy decisions) and the administrative responsibility of the director-general and the services (for the implementation of policy) should not be stretched too far" and that Commissioners should bear responsibility for what is going on in their services (see Committee of Independent Experts, First Report on Reform of the Commission: Analysis of current practice and proposals for tackling mismanagement, irregularities and fraud, 15 March 1999, point 9.3.4, p. 140). The Committee also stressed that ultimately "responsibility for all actions of the administration must find its way back to individual Commissioners and through them to the College. (…) The global operation of internal financial control falls within the concept of the collective responsibility of the Commission as a whole" (see Committee of Independent Experts, Second Report on Reform of the Commission: Analysis of current practice and proposals for tackling mismanagement, irregularities and fraud, 10 September 1999, Vol. I, point 4.9.5, pp. 118-119). The idea that Commissioners are responsible only for laying down policy, while Directors-General implement policy, was rejected as untenable both in law and in fact; a stance seen as paving the way to granting 'immunity' to Commissioners with respect to the sound implementation of policy and the efficient organisation of their services (see Ibid., Vol. II, points 7.9.1 and 7.9.6.).

151 See the European Parliament's Resolution of 27 April 2006 on the discharge for implementation of the European Union general budget for the financial year 2004 (para. 79). The issue has been first raised by the European Parliament in its Resolution of 4 April 2001 on the discharge for implementation of the European Union general budget for the financial year 1999. The Parliament asked in particular that each Commissioner signs an annual declaration of assurance that adequate internal controls have been put in place as well as a statement that, according to available information, all funds under his/her responsibility have been spent in accordance with the principles of sound and efficient management (see point 10.II). In its Resolution of 12 April 2005 (discharge for implementation of the European Union general budget for the financial year 2003), the Parliament invited "the Commission to convert the Annual Synthesis Report into a consolidated assurance statement on the Commission's management and financial controls as a whole" (para. 62). The issue has been recalled in discharge

Resolutions for subsequent financial years. Also the European Court of Auditors has recommended that the Commission, as an institution, adopt as its own Directors-General management representations' (see the *Annual Report concerning the financial year 2004*, para. 1.57).

[152] See European Parliament, Working Document of Mrs I. Grässle on Governance in the European Commission, Part 3, doc. 393.887, 30.8.2007, p. 2. Mrs Grässle has also expressed concern on the possibility of the European Commission and the college of Commissioners to remain accountable to the European Parliament "in the face of directorates-general acting with increasing independence and which in turn are granted discharge as an institution by Council and Parliament". She also observed that "directorates-general come across on their websites as being independent parts of the Commission, without having a corporate identity" and that implementing provisions for the same administrative procedures, subject to the same rules, can vary between different directorates-general (see European Parliament, Working Document of Mrs I. Grässle on Governance in the European Commission, Part 2, doc. 393.886, 30.8.2007, p. 2, 6 and 7). For example, along the same lines, in its discharge Resolution of 5 May 2010 concerning the financial year 2008 (see para. 319), the European Parliament highlighted the fact that the public regards the Commission as a single entity and regretted that only limited progress has been achieved in the formation of 'one-stop shops' covering the full range of Directorates-General responsible for research programmes.

[153] See European Commission, Report to the European Parliament on the follow-up to 2004 discharge decisions (summary) - European Parliament Resolutions, COM (2006) 641, 24.10.2006, p. 5, and the attached Commission Working Document, SEC(2006) 1376, p. 14. The Commission has pointed out that the "2000 reform centred on ensuring Authorising Officers by Delegation were solely responsible for the execution of their activities", with a division of management responsibilities between Directors-General and the collegiate structure (see European Commission, Report from the Commission to the European Parliament on the follow-up to 2005 discharge decisions (summary), COM(2007) 538, 19 September 2007, p. 6, and the attached Commission Working Document, SEC(2007) 1185, 19.9.2007, p. 17).

[154] See European Commission, "EU Budget - facts and myths", Press release Memo/07/350, 12.9.2007, p. 2. An implicit recognition of this argumentation is that Parliament normally granted discharge to the Commission, year after year. See box 14 "Postponing and refusing discharge to the Commission".

[155] See European Parliament, Resolution of 2 February 2006 on national management declarations, para 9. See also Parliament's resolutions of 12 April 2005 on the discharge for implementation of the European Union general budget for the financial year 2003 (para. 21); of 27 April 2006 on the discharge for implementation

of the European Union general budget for the financial year 2004 (para. 39); of 24 April 2007 on the discharge for implementation of the European Union general budget for the financial year 2005 (para. 23) and the Working Document by Mr Jan Mulder, "Redesigning accountability structures and control activities in the European Union", PE 378.567v01-00, 7.9.2006. The issue has also been examined in a study commissioned by the European Parliament, "Annual summaries in the context of shared management: evaluation, ways forward and possible usefulness for the Court of Auditors", 5.6.2009, doc. PE 411.270 (http://www.europarl.europa.eu/document/activities/cont/201005/20100519ATT74795/20100519ATT74795EN.pdf).

156 Such a 'four-pillar' scheme would be based on:

- annual *ex-ante* Disclosure Statements and *ex-post* declarations of assurance at the highest member state level;
- similar annual statements and declarations by each responsible authority at operational level (e.g. Managing Authority and Certifying Authority), supported by opinions from independent auditors;
- oversight by national authorities (in particular, Supreme Audit Institutions) over the control frameworks for EU funds and reporting on weaknesses in its design and operation in practice; and
- audit of the *ex-post* declarations of assurance by Supreme by Audit Institutions, or other independent audit bodies, and report to the national parliaments on the result.

(see European Commission, Communication on a roadmap to an integrated internal control framework, COM(2005) 252, 15.6.2005, p. 9). Parliament's appeal for an accrued role of national audit bodies intervened in 2006, where it called "on national audit bodies to assume responsibility for controlling the local use of EU funds, so as to make any consideration of establishing national offices of the Court of Auditors unnecessary" (see European Parliament, discharge Resolution of 27 April 2006 concerning the financial year 2004, para. 65). On the same issue see also Parliament's discharge Resolution of 24 April 2007 concerning the financial year 2005 (para. 28); discharge Resolution of 23 April 2009 concerning the financial year 2007 (para. 34); discharge Resolution of 5 May 2010 concerning the financial year 2008 (para. 53).

157 The Court stressed that such assurance very much depends on the reliability of the information supplied by beneficiaries when claiming EU funds (see European Court of Auditors, Opinion No. 6/2007 of 19 July 2007 on the annual summaries of member states, 'national declarations' of member states and audit work on EU funds of national audit bodies, Luxembourg, para. XI).

[158] See European Parliament, Resolution of 12 April 2005 containing the comments which are an integral part of the decision on the discharge for implementing the general budget of the European Union for the financial year 2003, Section III - Commission, para 27.

[159] The Parliament suggested that in place of one overall declaration, member states could issue a declaration for each major sector. The Parliament also suggested that instead of one signature from the Finance Minister, member states themselves should identify the relevant body at central level which should be responsible and accountable for issuing the declarations (see European Parliament, Resolution of 2 February 2006 on national management declarations, para 8; Resolution of 27 April 2006 on the discharge for implementation of the European Union general budget for the financial year 2004, paras 39-41; Resolution of 24 April 2007 on the discharge for implementation of the European Union general budget for the financial year 2005, paras. 23-24).

[160] See the Ecofin Council Conclusions, 13678/05, 8.11.2005, point 12.

[161] Thus, only one of the four pillars envisaged by the Commission is actually in place (see note 156): these are the statements and declarations from authorities at operational level, supported by opinions from independent auditors.

[162] A number of voluntary initiatives have been undertaken by some member states in the context of accountability to national parliaments on the use of shared management EU funds. For example, Denmark, the Netherlands, Sweden and the United Kingdom currently provide 'national declarations' that, although different in status, scope and content, are meant to provide an assessment of compliance on EU funds spent. One should also mention the reports and certificates of some national audit bodies on management of EU funds within their member states.

[163] See the Inter-institutional Agreement on budgetary discipline and sound financial management of 17 May 2006 between the European Parliament, the Council and the Commission, op. cit., Art. 44. It should be observed that when this commitment was translated into the Financial Regulation, a further adjustment eventually took place, by omitting a reference to the "assessment concerning the compliance of management and control systems". In the end, member states are only deemed to "produce an annual summary at the appropriate national level of the available audits and declarations" (see Art. 53(b)(3) of Council Regulation (EC, Euratom) No. 1605/2002, op. cit.). The Commission pointed out that a summary which is no more than a catalogue of available audits has no value added, and would make this a meaningless additional reporting exercise. Therefore, although recognising that this was not a legal requirement, the Commission invited member states to analyse the result from the information provided in the annual summary "in order to determine the implications at the level of the Member States as a

whole, highlighting any systemic deficiencies and summarising the main cross-cutting/horizontal issues, as well as indicating any further actions taken or to be taken as a consequence" (see European Commission, Guidance Note on the Annual Summary in relation to Structural Actions and the European Fisheries Fund, document COCOF 07/0063/06-EN, 12.11.2008, point 2.6.3 (http://www.europarl.europa.eu/document/activities/cont/200902/20090210ATT49079/20090210ATT49079EN.pdf). In its Opinion No. 6/2007 on the annual summaries of member states, 'national declarations' of member states, and audit work on EU funds of national audit bodies, the European Court of Auditors observed that the quality of the annual summaries will depend on the quality of the underlying declarations. If they highlight strengths and weaknesses they could stimulate improved control of the EU funds in shared management areas (see points III and IV, OJ C 216 of 14.9.2007, p. 3).

[164] See Parliament's Resolution of 5 May 2010 with comments forming an integral part of the decision on the discharge for implementation of the European Union general budget for the financial year 2008, Section III – Commission, point 43.

[165] See replies of Commissioner Samecki, in charge of Regional policy, to questions raised by the Parliament's budget control committee in the framework of the Discharge 2008, question 14 (http://www.europarl.europa.eu/document/activities/cont/200912/20091202ATT65755/20091202ATT65755EN.pdf). See also Commissioner Šemeta's speech on Discharge and Audit at the meeting of the Parliamentary Committee on Budgetary Control, 22 February 2010 (http://ec.europa.eu/commission_2010-2014/semeta/headlines/speeches/2010/02/cocobu_220210%20.pdf).

[166] See European Parliament resolution of 7 May 2009 on the development of the relations between the European Parliament and national parliaments under the Treaty of Lisbon, para 4.

[167] See European Parliament, discharge Resolution of 5 May 2010 concerning the financial year 2008 (paras. 49 and 51).

[168] In particular the proposal provides that annual summaries should also include an analysis of systematic or recurrent weaknesses as well as corrective actions taken or planned. National bodies should also provide a management declaration of assurance as to the completeness, accuracy and veracity of the accounts, the proper functioning of the internal control systems as well as to the legality and regularity of the underlying transactions and the respect of the principle of sound financial management. This should be accompanied by the opinion of an independent audit body (see COM (2010) 260, op. cit., Art. 53a(5), p. 74).

[169] See Art. 4(3) TEU.

170 As has been observed, "[t]he member states have a conflict of interest. On the one hand as members of the Council it is their duty in adopting regulations to create conditions for their implementation that are readily implemented and controlled by the Commission. On the other hand as nation states they favour their own systems of management and control. This hybrid arrangement leads to a lack of clarity on mutual responsibilities and obligations and fails to give any guarantee that the right balance has been struck in the interests of good management of Community monies" (see Committee of Independent Experts, Second Report on Reform of the Commission: Analysis of current practice and proposals for tackling mismanagement, irregularities and fraud, op. cit., Vol. I, para 3.5.3). It is worth noting that the Financial Regulation establishes the principle that "all financial actors and any other person involved in budget implementation, management, audit or control shall be prohibited from taking any action which may bring their own interests into conflict with those of the Communities" (see Art. 52(1) of Council Regulation (EC, Euratom) No. 1605/2002, op. cit.).

171 See European Court of Auditors, opinion No 2/2004 on the 'single audit' model, op. cit., para 24.

172 See note 202 for an illustration of the gap between irregularities detected by member states and those detected by the Commission.

173 See Joint Audit Strategy for Structural Actions (2007-2009), March 2007, p. 10.

174 See Art. 53b(2) and (3) of the Financial Regulation No. 1605/2002, op. cit.. The legal basis for Cohesion Policy 2007-13 recognises the principle at the basis of the Contract of Confidence, whereby the Commission can decide to rely principally on the opinion of the national audit authority with regard to the effective functioning of the systems and carry out its own on-the-spot audits in exceptional cases only (see Art. 73(3) of Regulation No 1083/2006, op. cit.).

175 A further example is provided by the possibility of 'partial closure' of operations in the Cohesion Policy (2000-06), introduced to make financial management more flexible. A partial closure of an operational programme is made conditional upon member states sending to the Commission a statement of expenditure and a declaration assessing the legality and regularity of the expenditure concerned. However, member states take the risk that if expenditure is found subsequently to be 'irregular' (for example following controls from the Commission or the Court of Auditors), this may lead to a net reduction of the EU financial contribution (no possibility to replace 'ineligible expenditure' with other expenditure, see later note 195). This risk of losing funds for the programme has recently led to an amendment of the rules to provide that "where irregularities in operations which have been subject to a declaration of partial closure are detected by the member state", EU funds released may be reused by the member state for

the operational programme concerned (see Art. 88(3) of Regulation No. 1083/2066, op. cit.). This implicitly means that national bodies could first certify compliance of the expenditure at partial closure, obtain on this basis the liquidation of EU funds by the Commission and undertake the control of expenditure afterwards. This potentially reverse the logic of the 'single audit' whereby member states, when introducing their reimbursement claims, certify their compliance with EU and national rules on the basis of adequate controls.

176 See note 42.

177 In the framework of the concept of 'tolerable risk of error' (see Box 7 "The cost of controls"), the Commission has pointed out that "in the shorter term, there needs to be a shared view among the Institutions on the extent to which it is reasonable to expect the Commission to limit the level of undetected error on an annual basis" (see European Commission, Synthesis of the Commission's management achievements in 2009, COM (2010) 281, 2.6.2010, p. 13). This stance finds some support in the Financial Regulation establishing that management of the risks relating to the legality and regularity has to take account of the "multi-annual character of programmes as well as the nature of the payments concerned." (see Art. 28a(2) of Council Regulation No 1605/2002, op. cit.). In this respect, the Council has emphasised "the multiannual character of EU expenditure, which should be duly taken into account. In this context, a transparent and reliable correction and recovery mechanism forms part of an efficient control framework. Furthermore, it considers that the effectiveness of controls should also be assessed on a multiannual perspective." (see Council recommendation in respect of the implementation of the budget for the financial year 2008, doc. 5826/10 Add 1, 3.2.2010, p. 7). As shown later (see note 201), programmes may still be uncleared ten years after the closure of a programming period.

178 See for example the Annual Activity Reports for the Year 2009, DG Agriculture and Rural Development, March 2010, p. 90; DG Regional Policy, 31.3.2010, p. 57; DG Employment, Social Affairs and Equal Opportunities, 30.3.2010, p. 68. Such reports are available at http://ec.europa.eu/atwork/synthesis/aar/index_en.htm.

179 See McCubbins & Schwartz (1984:65-179). Analogous to the use of real police patrols, the authors define "police-patrol oversight" as "centralised, active, and direct". This oversight is undertaken by the supervisory body "at its own initiative, with the aim of detecting and remedying any violations of legislative goals and, by its surveillance, discouraging such violations". By contrast, "fire-alarm oversight", in line with real fire alarms, is "less centralised and involves less active and direct intervention than police-patrol oversight". It is about "sniffing for fires", while "police-patrol oversight" is about placing "fire-alarm boxes on street corners",

building "neighbourhood fire houses" and sometimes dispatching the "hook-and-ladder" in response to an alarm. See also Brandsma (2007:3).

180 It is true that, for example in the Cohesion Policy, the *ex-ante* assessment by the Commission of national management and control systems and their audit strategy constitute the first essential building block of assurance on the design of the systems (see Figure 4). It remains the case, however, that this assessment is not a kind of 'stress test', as it is based on the description of these systems and not on their actual operation.

181 See Arts 53b(4) (shared management) and 53c(2) (decentralised management) of Council Regulation (EC, Euratom) No 1605/2002, op. cit.

182 The Commission has pointed out that financial corrections "provide a deterrent effect on Member States from any future mismanagement of EU funds - even where the funds remain within the Member States, the Member State must find the money to co-finance projects which replace those subject to financial corrections - and assist in eliminating errors detected during the implementation period, thereby reducing the residual risk of error at closure." (see European Commission, Impact of the action plan to strengthen the Commission's supervisory role under shared management of structural actions, COM (2010) 52, 18.2.2010, p. 12). Also, the Council has considered "that the application of suspension and correction mechanisms, whenever appropriate, acts as a deterrent and can thus have an important positive impact on the legality and regularity of expenditure" (see Council recommendation on the discharge to be given to the Commission in respect of the implementation of the general budget of the European Communities for the financial year 2007, doc. 5587/09 ADD 1 REV 1, 4.2.2009, page 25, point 3).

183 See Commission staff working document accompanying the report from the Commission to the European Parliament on the follow-up to 2007 discharge decisions, SEC (2009) 1427 final, 16.10.2009, p. 10. See also note 114.

184 For example, the Commission has challenged a number of irregularities uncovered by the Court on the basis that "the Commission does not consider that the circumstances identified by the Court provide a basis for the application of financial corrections" (see European Court of Auditors, Annual Report for the financial year 2008, reply of the Commission to the paragraph 6.17). This confirms that the 'benchmark' for compliance is actually provided by the rules on financial corrections.

185 The European Parliament wondered for example "if the current system of financial correction is sufficient to encourage Member States to combat fraud and irregularities" (see European Parliament - Resolution containing the comments which are an integral part of the decision on the discharge for implementing the general budget of the European Union for the financial year 2000, Section III -

Commission - 10 April 2002, point 78). More recently, Parliament has deplored "the fact that the system of sanctions for Member States returning high error rates and receiving large shares of funds is inefficient since they only repay between 3% and 5% of the overall appropriations in recoveries; it is concerned that the cost of maintaining proper control systems manifestly exceeds this amount, so that this is a negative incentive" (see European Parliament resolution of 5 May 2010 with observations forming an integral part of its Decisions on discharge in respect of the implementation of the European Union general budget for the financial year 2008, Section III - Commission and executive agencies, para. 119). The Court of Auditors observed that the financial corrections could provide no more "than a limited, auxiliary contribution to the necessary rigour of everyday management. Their effectiveness is essentially dependent on the number of checks performed. Furthermore, since financial corrections would intervene only after the fact, they could not be enough on their own to make good all the consequences of any transactions that might be implemented even though they did not meet the necessary regulatory requirements." (see European Court of Auditors - Opinion No 2/2005 on the proposal for a Council Regulation laying down general provisions on the European Regional Development Fund, the European Social Fund and the Cohesion Fund - paragraph 14, Official Journal C 121 of 20.5.2005, p. 14).

186 It should be noted however that the Court of Justice may, at the initiative of the Commission, impose a lump sum or penalty payment on a member state having failed to take the necessary measures to comply with a judgment of the Court (see Art. 260 TFEU).

187 Financial corrections may be limited to individual irregularities, or cover systemic errors or shortcomings in the national management or control systems. When it is not possible to quantify with precision the exact financial impact, extrapolated or flat-rate corrections are applied. The aim is to arrive at the best possible estimate of the financial impact on the EU budget. The amount of any correction is decided with respect to the principle of proportionality and the extent to which the fund was put at risk by individual irregularities or the shortcomings in the management or control systems.

188 See European Court of Auditors, Special report No. 7/2010 "Audit of the clearance of accounts procedure", answer of the Commission to para. IV (http://eca.europa.eu/portal/pls/portal/docs/1/5654728.PDF).

189 See European Court of Auditors, Annual report for the financial year 2006, Commission's reply to paragraph 5.76. Member states have an obligation of recovering undue payments to beneficiaries. EU rules provide that as a general rule any irregularity shall involve withdrawal of the wrongly obtained advantage

by a beneficiary (see Art. 4 of Regulation (EC, Euratom) No 2988/95 of the Council of 18 December 1995 on the protection of the European Communities financial interests, OJ L 312, 23.12.1995, p. 1). Similarly, the Financial Regulation (Art. 53b(2)(c)) requires member states to "recover funds wrongly paid or incorrectly used or funds lost as a result of irregularities or errors". As a matter of fact, in the period 2007-2009, member states recovered directly from beneficiaries less than 10% of the total amount of corrections outstanding at end 2006 for Agriculture (see DG "Agriculture and Rural development" Annual Activity Report for the year 2009, March 2010, p. 60, http://ec.europa.eu/atwork/synthesis/aar/doc/agri_aar.pdf). This is despite the fact that regulatory provisions (see Art. 32(2) of Regulation (EC) No 1290/2005) allow member states, as an incentive, to retain 20% of the amounts recovered and credited to the EU budget as flat rate recovery costs (except in cases of irregularity or negligence attributable to its administrative authorities or other official bodies). Rules provide that half of the cost (the other half is supported by the national budgets) of any undue payments not recovered by member states from the beneficiaries within four or, in the case of legal proceedings, eight years may be put at the charge of the EU budget. Member states are however obliged to pursue the recovery of undue amounts. In case of negligence, the Commission may decide to charge the entire outstanding amounts to the member states concerned (see Art. 32(5) of Regulation (EC) No 1290/2005). Concerning the Cohesion Policy, available data do not permit us to know the amounts of financial corrections and related recoveries applied by member states as a result of their own checks. This has recently lead Parliament to recall its previous requests in this respect (see European Parliament resolution of 22 April 2008 with observations forming an integral part of the decision on discharge in respect of the implementation of the European Union general budget for the financial year 2006, paras. 13, 110, 113, 116; and the resolution of 5 May 2010 with observations forming an integral part of the decision on discharge in respect of the implementation of the European Union general budget for the financial year 2008, para 32).

[190] According to the Financial Regulation (see Art. 96 of Regulation No 1605/2002, op. cit.), candidates or tenderers guilty of misrepresentation in supplying the information required by the contracting authority or failing to supply this information and contractors who have been declared to be in serious breach of their obligations under contracts covered by the budget may incur administrative or financial penalties. These shall be proportionate to the importance of the contract and the seriousness of the misconduct and may consist in:

a) the exclusion of the candidate or tenderer or contractor concerned from the contracts and grants financed by the budget, for a maximum period of ten years; and/or

b) the payment of financial penalties by the candidate or tenderer or contractor up to the value of the contract in question.

[191] The European Parliament, recalling "that the cost of financial corrections is borne by the Member States, usually by the taxpayer, rather than by the beneficiaries of the aid irregularly paid", has regretted "the lack of incentives for Member States to effectively control expenditure, since any ineligible expenditure identified by the Commission or the ECA can be substituted for eligible expenditure by a Member State". It asked the Commission "to make sure that in the future only irregularities identified by Member States themselves can be substituted for other expenditure without any loss of funding for the Member State concerned" (see European Parliament, Resolution of 22 April 2008 on the discharge for implementation of the European Union general budget for the financial year 2006, paragraphs 91 and 109). Parliament has reiterated a similar request in 2009 (see European Parliament, Resolution of 23 April 2009 on the discharge for implementation of the European Union general budget for the financial year 2007, para. 83).

[192] This is the case for the overwhelming part of corrections (around 80% in 2009) in direct agricultural spending, decided either by the Commission or member states.

[193] This is for example the case of milk quotas in Italy. Since 1984, cow's milk is marketed in the European Union on the basis of quotas initially introduced in order to achieve a balance between supply and demand and curb surpluses. Milk production quantities are broken down among the member states (national milk quotas) and among producers (individual quotas) in each member state. Where there is an overrun in the national quota, a surplus levy is payable by the producers. Regular production overruns have been recorded in Italy, with the subsequent request for payment of levies by the Commission. These corrections have been pre-financed by the national budget and their reimbursement by farmers is most problematic because of the protestations it regularly raises. In this respect the Court of Auditors has pointed out that for 2008 "Italy paid the levy for all producers concerned (€174.5 million) but only managed to collect €21.5 million from them" (see European Court of Auditors, Annual Report for the financial year 2008, op. cit., chap. 5, para. 5.22).

[194] See President Barroso's speech on the State of the Union 2010, 7.9.2010, SPEECH/10/411, p. 7.

[195]For Cohesion policy the practice distinguishes two types of financial corrections. The normal situation is that member states (on their own initiative or at the Commission's request) withdraw ineligible projects. They can thus re-use EU funding released from ineligible projects for other eligible expenditure (for example, new projects, see Council Regulation No. 1083/2006, Arts 98 to 100, op.

cit.). In the end, these corrections do not entail a net reduction of EU payments for the member state, provided that it has a sufficient buffer of eligible spending. However, if a member state refuses to withdraw the expenditure presented for reimbursement and considered ineligible by the Commission, the latter may apply financial corrections having the effect of a net reduction of EU payments.

[196] For example, for Agriculture, by the end of 2009, the 'conformity clearance' procedure was not complete for any year later than 2001. The financial accounts for 2009 show that for direct agriculture spending (EAGF), out of €462 million confirmed financial corrections in 2009, €274 million (or 58%) were actually recovered during the same year. This percentage is significantly lower for Structural and Cohesion Funds, where out of €2,411 million of confirmed financial corrections in 2009, only €478 million (or 20%) were actually recovered during the same year. In total, some €2.3 billion still remain to be recovered at year end 2009 (see European Commission, Annual accounts of the European Union, Financial Year 2009, SEC(2010) 963, 20.7.2010, pp. 81-95).

[197] See European Parliament, Resolution containing the comments which are an integral part of the decision on the discharge for implementing the general budget of the European Union for the financial year 2003, Section III - Commission, 12.4.2005, point 69.

[198] For example, the volume of financial corrections in the Cohesion policy has increased substantially in recent years. In 2009 an amount of €2.4 billion has been fixed, compared with €1.5 billion in 2008 and €288 million in 2007. At the end of 2009, cumulative corrections for Cohesion policy 1994-99 (€2.5 billion) were slightly less than half when compared to the cumulative amount so far for the 2000-06 period (€5.2 billion). The significant difference between the two programming periods (likely to be further amplified as the closure process for 2000-06 progresses) shows the extent of the margin of discretion enjoyed by the Commission in applying corrective mechanisms.

[199] For example, in response to the Court of Auditors' observations, the Commission has indicated that "[t]he findings presented by the Court show the situation at a particular point in the execution of these control processes. A large proportion of the errors are likely to be corrected through the operation of the multi-annual corrective system." (see European Court of Auditors, Annual report 2006, Commission's response to para. 1.41, OJ C 273 of 15.11.2007. See also European Commission, The control system for Cohesion Policy, How it works in the 2007–13 budget period, October 2009, p. 11).

[200] See European Court of Auditors, Opinion No 1/2010 "Improving the financial management of the European Union budget: Risks and challenges", 14.1.2010, point 7.

[201] For example, the Commission admits that for the closure of the 1994-99 programmes for Cohesion policy, there is still a high residual risk in a number of ERDF programmes (see DG "Regional policy" Annual Activity Report for the year 2009, 31.3.2010, p. 45, op. cit.)

[202] In this respect, out of the €625 million of total financial corrections and recoveries decided in 2009 for agriculture (EAGF), almost three-quarters originate from Commission's clearance actions and the rest from irregularities detected by member states. In 2008, 39% (or €360 million) of the financial corrections were detected by member states (see European Commission, Annual accounts of the European Union, Financial Year 2009, SEC(2010) 963, 20.7.2010, p. 81). Concerning Cohesion policy, the Court of Auditors has observed in its last Annual report that at least almost a third of the errors found could have been detected and corrected by member states before certifying expenditure to the Commission (see European Court of Auditors, Annual report on the implementation of the 2009 budget, 9.9.2010, op. cit., para. 4.23).

[203] The 'conformity clearance' exercise in Agriculture cannot exclude from EU financing national expenditure made more than 24 months before the Commission officially notifies the member state of its audit findings (see Art. 31(4)(a) of Regulation (EC) No 1290/2005). The Commission has repeatedly proposed an extension of this time limit, but these proposals were turned down by both the Council and the European Parliament. In the Cohesion policy, national authorities are required to keep available supporting documents regarding expenditure and audits for a period of three years following the closure of an operational programme or part of it, except in the case of legal proceedings or at the duly motivated request of the Commission (see Art. 90 of Regulation No. 1083/2006, op. cit).

[204] See "Introduction" by Heinrich Aigner, Vice-Chairman of the Committee on Budgets (European Parliament, 1973, point 12).

[205] The routine occurrence of corrective mechanisms is also shown by the fact that the EU financial statements disclose each year as a contingent asset an amount of expenditure, based on exclusions in previous years, which is likely to be discarded from EU financing by future clearance decisions (this represents an amount of €3.9 billion for Agriculture and Cohesion spending at year-end 2009). This entry in the accounts could actually be interpreted as a 'performance indicator' and even as a target for the Directorates-General concerned, while representing at the same time a 'negative' indicator for the policy objectives.

[206] See European Commission, Annual accounts of the European Union, Financial Year 2009, SEC(2010) 963, 20.7.2010, p. 83.

[207] See Council recommendation in respect of the implementation of the budget for the financial year 2008, doc. 5826/10 Add 1, 3.2.2010, p. 26. Indeed, Cohesion policy is based on the principle that local authorities can put in place a programme of actions because funds are ensured for a number of years. Reducing the availability of the funds would not serve the purpose of the policy. One may also notice that the non-observance of the principle of additionality (a principle providing that contributions from the Structural Funds shall not replace public or equivalent structural expenditure by a member state) triggers the application of financial corrections, with the Commission cancelling all or part of the Structural Funds contribution to the member state concerned (see Art. 99(5) of the Regulation No 1083/2006, op. cit.). The impact would be again to reduce further the funds available, which is at odds with the aim of the policy.

[208] Arts 310 (5) and 317 TFEU.

[209] See note 92.

[210] See note 80.

[211] See D. Hübner (2007a:3).

[212] See Commissioner Šemeta's speech on Discharge and Audit at the meeting of the Parliamentary Committee on Budgetary Control, 22 February 2010, op. cit.

[213] See Art. 60(1) of the Financial Regulation, Council Regulation (EC, Euratom) No 1605/2002, op. cit.

[214] See Art. 60(7) of the Financial Regulation, Council Regulation (EC, Euratom) No 1605/2002, op. cit.

[215] See European Commission, The annual reports and declarations required of Directors-General under the reform of the Commission, doc. SEC (2001) 875/6, 27.6.2001, point 2.2.1. For example, one can read in the 2008 Annual Activity Report for DG Regional Policy that outputs and results reported "relate to activity which is primarily the responsibility of the Member States, given the shared management responsibilities of Cohesion policy. It is not a direct measure of the performance of DG Regional Policy" (see DG Regional Policy's Annual Activity Report for the year 2008, 31.3.2009, point 1.2.1.3, p. 11 (http://ec.europa.eu/atwork/synthesis/aar/aar2008/doc/regio_aar.pdf). The same concept is repeated in the Annual Management Plan for 2010 (see DG Regio annual management plan, 10.5.2010, p. 19 (http://ec.europa.eu/atwork/synthesis/amp/doc/regio_mp.pdf).

[216] See for example the Annual Activity Reports for the Year 2009, DG Agriculture and Rural Development, March 2010, p. 90; DG Regional Policy, 31.3.2010, p. 57; DG Employment, Social Affairs and Equal Opportunities, 30.3.2010, p. 68.

[217] As required by Art. 60(7) of the Financial Regulation, Council Regulation (EC, Euratom) No. 1605/2002, op. cit. It is worth recalling that the origin of this

provision can be found in the White Paper for reform of the Commission presented by the latter in 2000. "Action 82" stated that "[b]y signing the annual report, the Director-General takes responsibility for the accuracy and completeness of the information presented" (see European Commission, *Reforming the Commission*, White Paper, COM (2000) 200, vol. II, 5.4.2000, pp. 61-62).

218 See Commission decision C(2010)1858 of 8 April 2010, Annex IV, Charter of tasks and responsibilities of authorising officers by delegation, Model declaration by the authorising officer by delegation relating to the Annual Activity Report, p. 9. It should be observed however that such footnote has been inserted in some annual activity reports (see for example the Annual Activity Reports for the Year 2009 - DG Regional Policy, 31.3.2010, p. 57; DG Research, 26.3.2010, p. 60) but not in others (see for example, DG Agriculture and Rural Development, March 2010, p. 90 and DG Employment, Social Affairs and Equal Opportunities, 30.3.2010, p. 68).

219 See European Commission, 2010 Preliminary Draft Budget, Volume 0, General introduction, p. 15. The Budget Memorandum is based on information from the 'Activity statements' which, with the introduction of activity-based budgeting, constitute the main instrument for justifying the appropriations requested by the Commission. The 'Activity statements' are meant to present performance information for each area of EU activity, providing the main elements justifying the level of resources requested by the Commission in its preliminary draft budget. The statements should include details of the resources allocated to the activities, as well as associated objectives, indicators, outputs and outcomes.

220 See European Commission, 2010 Preliminary Draft Budget, Introduction, point 2.1.

221 See European Commission, 2010 Preliminary Draft Budget, Volume 0, op. cit., p. 15.

222 See European Commission, 2010 Preliminary Draft Budget, Budget Memorandum, "Re-launching the EU's economic activity", p. 3.

223 See Oliver, D. (1995), *Standards of Conduct in Public Life – What Standards?*, Public Law, p. 497, cited in Harlow (2002b:10).

224 For example, although taking 1/3 of the EU budget resources, Cohesion policy is still a relatively small policy when compared to similar spending in member states. Another example is provided by the research domain, whose bulk of public funding is provided by national budgets (around 95%).

225 See note 81.

226 It is worth mentioning in this respect that the Inter-Institutional Agreement provides that "[t]he institutions will, as far as possible, avoid entering items in the budget involving insignificant amounts of expenditure on operations (see the

Inter-Institutional Agreement on budgetary discipline and sound financial management of 17 May 2006 between the European Parliament, the Council and the Commission, op. cit., para. 33).

227 See European Court of Auditors, Opinion No. 1/2010, "Improving the financial management of the European Union budget: Risks and challenges", 14.1.2010, para. 14.

228 EU priorities for the Cohesion policy are multiple and wide-ranging ("sustainable development by strengthening growth, competitiveness, employment and social inclusion and by protecting and improving the quality of the environment"). The priority convergence objective seeks to improve "conditions for growth and employment through the increasing and improvement of the quality of investment in physical and human capital, the development of innovation and of the knowledge society, adaptability to economic and social changes, the protection and improvement of the environment, and administrative efficiency." A wide remit is also envisaged for the other two objectives, "Regional competitiveness and employment" and "European territorial cooperation" (see Council Regulation (EC) No. 1083/2006, Art. 3, op. cit.). The Barca report on an agenda for a reformed Cohesion policy observes: "In the absence of a high-level cultural and political compromise on a policy model, strategies, both at EU and Member States (Regions) level, often lack clear-cut objectives and a justification of how planned interventions should achieve them. Priorities are very broad, covering all possible areas of public action and cannot be identified with any European public good" (European Commission, 2009:106).

229 This refers to the usual relationship *input⇒ output⇒ outcome⇒ impact*. The following definitions are given by the "Glossary of Key Terms in Evaluation and Results Based Management" (see OECD, Development Assistance Committee, Paris, 2002). Inputs (The financial, human, and material resources used for the development intervention); Outputs (The products, capital goods and services which result from a development intervention; may also include changes resulting from the intervention which are relevant to the achievement of outcomes); Outcomes (The likely or achieved short-term and medium-term effects of an intervention's outputs); Impacts (Positive and negative, primary and secondary long-term effects produced by a development intervention, directly or indirectly, intended or unintended).

230 The word "conditionality" is typically employed in the context of the International Monetary Fund (IMF), where it is used to specify "how the Fund's financing will be linked to the member's implementation of an adequate program of policy adjustments in response to its external imbalances" (see International Monetary Fund, Guidelines on Conditionality, 25.9.2002, point 1, p. 8). In

particular "[a]ll conditionality under an IMF-supported program must be 'macro-critical', that is to say, either critical to the achievement of program goals or for monitoring implementation, or necessary for the implementation of specific provisions under the IMF's Articles of Agreement". This means that IMF disbursements are made conditional upon demonstrable policy actions (see International Monetary Fund, Factsheet on IMF conditionality, September 2009 (http://www.imf.org/external/np/exr/facts/conditio.htm).

231 See European Commission (2010), *Ex-Post Evaluation of Cohesion Policy Programmes 2000-2006 financed by the European Regional Development Fund in Objective 1 and 2 Regions*, Synthesis Report, op. cit., p. 11.

232 Ibid., p. 162. It is interesting to note that the same remark was made some years ago. A study indicates that "While there is universal agreement about the need for monitoring as an important dimension to accountability, there is little evidence that the outcomes of the monitoring system are being fed back into the management process" (see European Commission, DG Regional Policy, *A Study of the Efficiency of the Implementation Methods for Structural Funds*, December 2003). One may recall in this respect concerns previously expressed by the Council and its intention to ensure that "assistance will be allocated where appraisal shows medium term economic and social benefits commensurate with the resources deployed. Operations should be adjusted to accord with the results of monitoring and evaluation." (see European Council, Presidency Conclusions of the European Council in Edinburgh, Future Financing of the Community, Delors II package, 11-12 December 1992).

233 Although it is admitted that a direct casual link is difficult to establish, for example, between ERDF assistance and expected developments in terms of GDP growth rates and unemployment (see DG Regio Activity Based Statement for the 2010 draft Budget, p. 6). A similar conclusion is drawn in the Commission staff working document on the Budget review (SEC(2010)7000, op. cit., p. 25).

234 See European Court of Auditors, Opinion No. 1/2010 "Improving the financial management of the European Union budget: Risks and challenges", 14.1.2010, par. 16.

235 See European Parliament, Resolution containing the comments which are an integral part of the decision on the discharge for implementing the general budget of the European Union for the financial year 2003, Section III - Commission, 12.4.2005, point 32(d).

236 See European Parliament, Resolution of 12 July 2007 on the role and effectiveness of Cohesion policy in reducing disparities in the poorest regions of the EU, point H.

[237] See European Commission, Synthesis of the Commission's management achievements in 2007, COM (2008) 338, 4.6.2008, p. 2.

[238] Ibid., p. 2.

[239] To borrow an expression used by Advocate General Darmon in his conclusions concerning Case-law 16/88, Commission/Council, op. cit., ECR 1989, p. 3472.

[240] For example, none of the 37 actions undertaken by the "action plan to strengthen the Commission's supervisory role under shared management of structural actions" (see COM(2008) 97, 19.2.2008) has covered specifically 'value for money' issues. And the Commission's services in charge for Cohesion policy are reported having "neither sufficient availability of resources nor the special expertise in the field to undertake performance audits in the near future" (see D. Hübner, 2007a:2).

[241] See Art. 319(1) TFEU. In the founding treaties it was up to the Council to grant discharge to the Commission. Later, with the 1970 Budget Treaty (Treaty of Luxembourg of 22.04.1970, OJ L 2 of 2.1.1971), discharge was granted jointly by the Council and Parliament. Since June 1977, with the entering into force of the Treaty of Brussels (22.7.1975, OJ L 359 of 31.12.1977), granting discharge to the Commission has become a prerogative of the European Parliament.

[242] See Art. 319 (2) TFEU. It is to be observed that this provision (as well as the following sub-paragraph) only refers to expenditure, not to revenue, which is ensured through national contributions and is basically member states' game preserve. Parliament has only a consultative power on revenue arrangements (see note 61).

[243] See note 140.

[244] See Art. 15 of the Declaration of the Rights of Man and the Citizen (National Assembly of France, 26 August 1789).

[245] European Parliament resolution on reform of budgetary control procedures and institutions, 13.12.2000, para. E.

[246] Ibid., para. D.

[247] See Art. 234 TFEU. The members of the Commission shall resign as a body if the motion of censure is carried by a two-thirds majority of the votes cast, representing a majority of the members of the European Parliament. However, this provision is only an "emergency break" and not a mechanism for accountability. There have been only eight motions of censure and no one has ever been adopted.

[248] See European Court of Auditors, Opinion No. 2/2005 of 18 March 2005 (op. cit.), para. 6.

[249] See European Parliament, discharge Resolution of 5 May 2010 concerning the financial year 2008 (para. H).

[250] See note 40.

[251] See the Treaty amending certain financial provisions, signed in Brussels on 22 July 1975, preamble.

[252] See European Parliament, discharge Resolution of 5 May 2010 concerning the financial year 2008 (para. 70).

[253] See Ecofin Council Conclusions on the budget guidelines for 2011 adopted on 16 March 2010, doc. 6794/10, 24 February 2010, p. 9.

[254] See European Commission (2002:19).

[255] See note 68.

[256] This principle goes back to the Magna Carta (1215), which is at the origin of modern constitutional principles.

[257] The Commission further explains that the 'democratic deficit' is usually meant to suggest the lack of full parliamentary scrutiny by and accountability to the European Parliament; presently, the term is used to indicate a manifestation of this in the form of the incomplete monitoring and control of the budget by the citizens (see European Commission (1998, annex 2, p. 3).

[258] See in this respect European Commission (2010), *Ex-Post Evaluation of Cohesion Policy Programmes 2000-2006 financed by the European Regional Development Fund in Objective 1 and 2 Regions*, Synthesis Report, op. cit., pp. 159-161.

[259] This refers to the SMART standard provided for by Art. 27(3) of the Financial Regulation No. 1605/2002, op. cit.

[260] M. Power (1997:147), cited in Schenker-Wicki (2006).

[261] In this respect, although they may provide useful additional information depending on the scope and quality of the work that underlies them, 'national declarations' do not seem to bring a definitive solution. They respond to national motives; their status, scope and content is different and it seems unrealistic to standardise it. They constitute in practice a self-assessment by member states, not necessarily based on conclusive evidence, of how eligibility rules have been complied with (therefore 'value for money' remains outside their scope).

[262] See Auditor General of Canada (2002:10).

[263] See European Commission, President José Manuel Barroso's political guidelines for the next Commission, op. cit., p. 36.

[264] The draft document (dated 6.10.2009) suggested that most of the EU budget should be spent on three key areas (namely, sustainable growth and jobs; energy and tackling climate change; and Europe in the world). This would imply either an overall increase in EU spending (a hypothesis not really in line with the *air du temps* amidst the economic crisis) or, most likely, a corresponding (significant)

reduction for the traditional high-budget areas like Agriculture and Cohesion policy. The proposal envisaged a radical reduction of Agriculture spending, particularly direct aid and market intervention mechanisms. Spending would also, to a large extent, become national again, especially for the co-funding of direct aid. Concerning the Cohesion policy, the draft suggested increasing the concentration, conditionality and performance. As a result, most of the regions currently benefiting from Cohesion policy would be excluded from it, precluding to a re-nationalisation of this policy. The document is available at http://www.euractiv.com/pdf/Draft%20document%20reforming%20the%20budget%20oct%202009.pdf.

265 See for example the idea of setting up a European Energy Community to meet the challenges of climate change, energy security and the economic crisis launched by J. Delors according to whom, if necessary, the project could initially be achieved by an initial core group of dedicated member states through the shape of strengthened cooperation as defined by Art. 20 TEU. Mr Delors recalls that a differentiated approach of this kind has been used in the past to make major strides in the European project like the Schengen area and the single currency. The report "Towards a European Energy Community: A Policy Proposal", April 2010, is available at http://www.notre-europe.eu/uploads/tx_publication/Etud76-Energy-en.pdf. See also in this connection the declaration "Towards a new European Energy Community" subscribed by Mr Buzek, President of the European Parliament, and Mr Delors (http://www.notre-europe.eu/uploads/tx_publication/EN_Buzek-Delors_declaration.pdf).

266 See European Council, *Financial Perspective 2007-2013,* 15915/05, Brussels, 19 December 2005, para 2bis.

267 Ibid., para 80.

268 See Art. 1 TEU. The concept is reaffirmed by Art. 10(3) TEU. See also note 70.

269 See Preamble of the Treaty on European Union.

270 One should also mention that the provisions of the new Treaty (Arts 290 and 291 TFEU) put the Council and Parliament as co-legislators on an equal footing in relation to the conferral of delegated and implementing powers to the Commission.

271 See Art. 17 (8) TEU.

272 See Art. 318 TFEU.

273 The European Parliament decided in June 2010 to set up a special committee on the policy challenges and budgetary resources for a sustainable European Union after 2013. This committee should in particular define Parliament's political priorities in both legislative and budgetary terms, estimate how much money the

EU will need to achieve its objectives and the related policies, draw up guidelines on how resources should be distributed, and propose how the EU budget should be financed in the future. The mandate of the committee will last until the Commission presents its proposal with figures for the next multi-annual financial framework, planned for July 2011.

[274] See European Parliament resolution of 29 March 2007 on the future of the European Union's own resource, point 34. Also, in its resolution of 25 March 2009 on the Mid-Term Review of the 2007-2013 Financial Framework, Parliament pointed out that the reform of revenue and a review of expenditure "should be run in parallel with the aim of merging them in a global and integrated reform for a new system of EU financing and spending at the latest for the MFF starting in 2016/2017" (see para. 9).

[275] See European Parliament resolution of 8 June 2005 on Policy Challenges and Budgetary Means of the enlarged Union 2007-2013, point 7.

[276] See European Parliament resolution of 25 March 2009 on the Mid-Term Review of the 2007-2013 Financial Framework, points 11, 12, 16. Parliament has also expressed concern (stressing the contradiction with the basic principles of the reform of 2000 following the White Paper) on the fact that the present budgetary cycle "tends to add one priority after another without taking any political decision as to issues that, given the limited resources available from the tax-payer, need to be scaled down in order to give way to the most crucial priorities" (see European Parliament resolution of 25 March 2009 on the ABB-ABM method as a management tool for allocating budgetary resources, para 13). Parliament has recently acknowledged "that the current economic climate might lead the budgetary authority to make some efforts towards reprioritisation within the budget in order to ensure the adequate funding of priorities (...)" (see European Parliament, Resolution of 22 September 2010 on the proposal for a Council regulation laying down the multiannual financial framework for the years 2007-2013, point vi).

[277] See European Parliament resolution of 24 April 2007 with comments forming an integral part of the decision on the discharge for implementation of the European Union general budget for the financial year 2005, Section III - Commission, points 205 and 238.

[278] See European Parliament, Resolution accompanying the decision concerning discharge in respect of the implementation of the general budget of the European Union for the 2002 financial year, 21.4.2004, point 4.

[279] See Art. 211 of the Treaty establishing the European Community (TEC) and Art. 17(1) TEU.

[280] See Arts 3 TEU, 13(1) TEU and 7 TFEU.

[281] See Art. 317 TFEU.

[282] See Art. 17(1) TEU, emphasis added. See also note 83.

[283] See Letter by President Barroso to the Members of the European Parliament, 7 September 2010, MEMO/10/393.

[284] See European Commission, "Reforming the Budget, Changing Europe" (SEC(2007) 1188, 12.9.2007, point 2) and the summary of the experts' contributions (SEC(2008) 2739, 3.11.2008, point 2). It is worth mentioning that an attempt to determine what the EU should be doing had been made by the Commission by identifying some criteria, such as "economies of scale", the "need of a comprehensive approach with other EU financed policies" or of "lightening the burden on national budgets". These criteria, however, were too vague to be made operational (See European Commission, Global appraisal of the budgetary problems of the Community, COM(78) 64, Brussels, 27 February, pp. 6-8). President Barroso has recently stated the need to "develop a much clearer doctrine of how we decide when action needs to be taken at EU level" (see European Commission, Political guidelines for the next Commission, op. cit., p. 39). The European Court of Auditors has suggested that "[t]he concept of European added value should be articulated in a suitable political declaration or in EU legislation in order to provide guidance to the EU's political authorities to be used when choosing expenditure priorities" (See European Court of Auditors, Opinion No 1/2010 "Improving the financial management of the European Union budget: Risks and challenges", 14.1.2010, point 18). Tarschys (2005) examines the concept of EU added value and its use in various policy settings, suggesting some ways to convert it from an all-purpose argument into a better tool for policy choices.

[285] See Arts 3 TEU, 5(1) TEU and 311 TFEU.

[286] See Art. 5(3) TEU.

[287] See Art. 5 of the protocol on subsidiarity/proportionality attached to the Treaty of Lisbon. The Financial Regulation No 1605/2002, op. cit., establishes a link between 'value for money' and the setting of performance indicators in such a way that results can be assessed for each activity (see 'whereas' No 11 and Art. 27 (3)).

[288] See European Commission, "Reforming the Budget, Changing Europe" (SEC(2007) 1188, 12.9.2007, p. 5.

[289] This was one of the key assumptions underlying the Commission's proposal concerning the 2007-13 financial framework (see European Commission, Communication on the Financial Perspective 2007-13, COM(2004) 487, 14.7.2004, page 5).

[290] As pointed out by J. Pelkmans, cited in Public Finances in the EU, Conference organised by the Bureau of European Policy Advisers of the European

Commission, 3-4 April 2008, Brussels, p. 25 (proceedings available at http://ec.europa.eu/dgs/policy_advisers/publications/docs/public_finances_web_version_en.pdf).

[291] See J. Monnet, (1978:316).

[292] Reflection Group on the Future of the EU 2030, Report to the European Council by the Reflection Group, May 2010, p. 5.

[293] For example the Council has taken the view that no increase of resources is needed for the current 2007-13 financial framework (see Ecofin Council conclusions on the budget guidelines for 2011 adopted on 16 March 2010, op. cit., p. 3). By contrast, Parliament has considered that needs cannot be met through redeployment or reprioritisation and that a revision of the multi-annual financial framework and of the flexibility mechanisms is necessary (see European Parliament, Resolution of 22 September 2010 on the proposal for a Council regulation laying down the multiannual financial framework for the years 2007-2013, point vii). A modification of the financial framework requires unanimity by the Council and the consent of the European Parliament (see Box 2 "An overview of the EU's financial frameworks").

[294] See President Barroso's speech on the State of the Union 2010, 7.9.2010, SPEECH/10/411, p. 6.

[295] In this respect Parliament's stance is that there is a need for "prior identification of positive and negative priorities rather than through self-imposed ceilings" (see European Parliament resolution of 25 March 2009 on the Mid-Term Review of the 2007-2013 Financial Framework, para 11).

[296] For example, as noted by Parliament, "a large proportion of the Union's objectives have been taken into account by the Member States in their national budgets" (see European Parliament resolution of 25 March 2009 on the Mid-Term Review of the 2007-2013 Financial Framework, para 18). Parliament also noted that since the EU budget is very limited compared to national budgets there is a need to create synergies between the EU budget and national budgets in order to implement common EU strategies. It stressed that coherence gives European policies greater impact, achieving true European added value while supporting long-term policy objectives (see European Parliament resolution of 15 June 2010 on the mandate for the trilogue on the 2011 draft budget, para. 15).

[297] In this respect, president Barroso has indicated that where the added value of EU action can't be demonstrated, the Commission will support reductions. He has also stressed that spending on the right policies only makes real sense if it secures the desired results on the ground (see Statement of President Barroso on the budget review, 19 October 2010).

[298] J. Monnet, (1978:127).

[299] See European Commission President José Manuel Barroso, Political guidelines for the next Commission, op. cit., p. 29.

[300] This logic is intrinsic in the concept of "value for money" set by Art. 27(3) of the Financial Regulation No. 1605/2002, op. cit.

[301] As an example, the Council recognises "the need to concentrate operations in regions on a limited number of priorities to ensure they have a tangible impact" (see Council conclusions on the Strategic report of 2010 by the Commission on the implementation of the Cohesion policy programmes, Press release, 14 June 2010, p. 3).

[302] Gros (2008:17) argues that it should be easier to reach agreement on sunset clauses than on an explicit agreement to lower expenditure today, because a sunset clause's impact is uncertain and lies in the future, thus generating much less opposition. Sunset clauses are a recognised element of good governance for reform. Organisational theory, empirical studies and experience all show that once a specific structure has been established, those who hold positions in the structure have a natural tendency to make it survive and grow even if it does not seem reasonable to outsiders (see Sigma 2007:34). Some kind of sunset clauses exist already in the current legislative framework, although 'performance' is very much dependent on the 'spending' rate rather than on achieving pre-determined results. For example, in the Cohesion policy, funds are de-committed if not used after a certain period (n+2 rule).

[303] See COM (2010) 700, op. cit, pp. 5-6.

[304] According to the proposal, the payment of the grants would be entirely based on the assessment of outputs/results, thus putting in place the conditions for a shift of the control efforts from the financial to the scientific side (See European Commission, "Simplifying the implementation of the Research Framework Programmes", COM(2010)187, 29.4.2010, point 3.3, p. 10). A similar stance is taken by the Commission in its conclusions of the fifth report on economic, social and territorial cohesion (see COM (2010) 642, 9.11.2010), where the Commission delineates the future of Cohesion policy with a concentration of financial resources, the introduction of conditionality and incentives and a focus on results.

[305] See Auditor General of Canada (2002:5).

[306] See SEC(2007) 1188 final, 12.9.2007, p. 10.

[307] See Art. 17(1) TEU.

[308] See European Commission President José Manuel Barroso, Political guidelines for the next Commission, op. cit., p. 39.

[309] It is referred here to the general principles of EU law as stated by the EU Court of Justice (see for example Case-law No. 10/56, Meroni & Co., Industrie

Metallurgiche, società in accomandita semplice v High Authority of the European Coal and Steel Community, Judgment of the Court of 13 June 1958, ECR. 1958, p. 157). A delegation of powers can only involve clearly defined executive powers, the use of which must be entirely subject to the supervision by the delegating authority. As observed by the Court of Justice, since it replaces the choices of the delegator by the choices of the delegate, a delegation of powers implying a wide margin of discretion brings about an actual transfer of responsibility. Similarly, the Financial Regulation No 1605/2002, op. cit. (see Art. 54(1)) provides that "the implementing tasks delegated must be clearly defined and fully supervised as to the use made of them", the delegation "shall comply with the principle of sound financial management" and no implementing tasks "may give rise to conflicts of interests". In the event of shared management, this will require for example to re-establish the principle that the Commission "shall first carry out document and on-the-spot checks into the existence, relevance and proper operation within the entities to which it entrusts implementation, in accordance with the rules of sound financial management" of the procedures applied, of control systems, of accounting systems and procurement and grant award procedures. And shall review such arrangements periodically (see Box 4 "Systems assessment").

310 In its conclusions on the EU budget review the Commission puts forward the idea of a 'Development and Investment Partnership Contract' between the Commission and the member states, setting out the objectives to be achieved, how progress towards the achievement of these objectives will be quantified and measured and the allocation of national and EU resources among priority areas and programmes. Also, the Commission identifies the institutional capacity at national, regional and local level as key for successful development, implementation and monitoring of the policies. The allocation of EU financial resources should therefore take account of the capacity to effectively utilise these resources (see COM (2010) 700, op. cit, p. 14).

311 Because of the national co-financing and/or because these bodies often manage other national funds.

312 This refers to the concept of 'fire alarm' versus 'police patrol' oversight discussed in note 179.

313 For example, this would imply re-establishing a systematic presence of the Commission on the ground, for example in the 'monitoring committees' on Cohesion policy which are in charge of assessing the effectiveness and quality of the implementation of operational programmes, by reviewing progress made towards achieving the specific targets and proposing suitable measures. This was the case in the previous programming period, while today the Commission's

presence is optional (see Art. 64(2)) of Council Regulation (EC) No. 1083/2006, op. cit.).

[314] See Art. 60(1) and (7) of the Financial Regulation n° 1605/2002, op. cit.

[315] See Art. 318 TFEU.